Real Life Rituals

Real
Life
Rituals

Karyl Huntley

Spiritual Living Press
Burbank, California

Second printing—2007

Copyright © 2005 by Karyl Huntley

Spiritual Living Press
2600 West Magnolia Boulevard
Burbank, CA 91505

Printed in the United States of America.
ISBN13 978-0-9727184-6-2
ISBN 0-9727184-6-X
Library of Congress Control Number: 2005926507

Design by Randall Friesen

*Dedicated to
Michael and Melanie
who came to earth
through the doorway
in me. Blessed be.*

. Contents .

Part Three

The Transitions of Life

Part Four
The Wheels

. *Acknowledgments* .

I am so grateful for each and every event and person that helped define the pathway to the creation of this book. My love of ritual became conscious in my women's group, EGGS; thank you to my sisters there. Thank you to the wild and wonderful women of the various WomanSpirit committees through the years, as well as all the women who attended the WomanSpirit retreats. Thank you to the United Church of Religious Science which, for several years, allowed me to be Ritual Coordinator for national meetings. Thank you to all my teachers, my students, and my congregants who have seen me burn more paper, slosh more holy water, and lead them through more vows than they could ever imagine.

Specific thanks go to my editor Randall Friesen, my publisher Rodney Scott, and the wonderful staff at Spiritual Living Press. Thank you to my music angel Dr. Karen Drucker. Thank you to Dr. Lloyd George Tupper, Rev. Mary Murray Shelton, and Rev. Barbara Leger for years of support and inspiration. Thank you to Jay Gustafson and Eileen McCann who helped me in the creation of the Boys Coming of Age Ritual. Thank you to Kate McCarthy, who reminds me I can do an instant ritual whenever I need it, even at a bus stop. Thank you to SueZee Poinsett for helping me get started, and to Rev. Joyce Dufalla, who kept asking me, "How's it coming?"

Thank you to my darling family, mom Doris, son Michael, and daughter Melanie for their love and unconditional support. You are so precious to me.

Lastly, thank you to my readers, who I now ask to join me for a brief ritual of acknowledgment.

Place your hand on your heart right now, and take a deep breath. Let the world around you dissolve as you read the following words aloud:

"I acknowledge myself as a unique and sacred being in all the realms of time, space, and any other dimensions. I acknowledge myself for choosing to come to this beautiful earth to learn and prosper. From this moment forward, I trust the holy life within me to lead me into deep experiences of spiritual satisfaction and into the paradise that is already mine.

"Blessed be."

Introduction to Real Life Rituals

Real Life Rituals is for those of you who wish to deepen your experience of life and to enhance your relationship to the sacred, to the seasons, to life passages, and to each other.

We live in a deep and sacred mystery that cannot be fully understood intellectually but can be experienced when we open ourselves to the flow of life in and through us. This mystery is safe, supportive, and unifying. It overflows with beauty, wisdom, and spiritual direction. We can more easily access the mystery when we sink into it, rather than think about it.

Ritual does just that. Sinking you into the mystery of life, its power lies beyond the words that are spoken or the ceremonial objects that are used. It allows you to see the ways that we are all the same and the ways in which we are unified with life. In addition to teaching respect for your own path, reverence for all living beings, faith in natural cycles, and comfort with the unseen side of life, rituals allow you to viscerally experience respect, reverence, faith, and comfort.

Our lives are rife with changes, some disappointing and others joyful. Our loved ones pass on; our children grow up and leave home; our jobs and health challenge us. We experience so much on a superficial level and then wonder why life doesn't hold more meaning for us. Rituals help us tap in to the greater depths of feeling, meaning, and belonging that life has for us.

Drawing on myth, fable, and religion—traditions that have been with us for ages—*Real Life Rituals* offers you celebrations for the seasons of the year as well as the transitions of your life. You may choose to perform the rituals exactly as they appear in the book, using the words as your script, or you may use the text as a general outline for your own personal, unique celebration. You may decide to use a section of one ritual with pieces of other ceremonies to create an entirely new ritual for a unique and specific occasion. Regardless of how many celebrants participate, these rituals can be adapted for use by an individual, a family, a small group or a large gathering.

Part One of *Real Life Rituals* offers information about the various elements that make up a ritual. Use it as a reference when you wish to create your own special ceremonies.

Part Two contains rituals that celebrate the seasons of the year.

In Part Three you will find rites-of-passage rituals for the transitions of your life.

Lastly, Part Four contains a series of wheel illustrations that depict the flow of energy commemorated by the rituals of the book.

You *can* feel more completely connected to your life today. Your life can be richer and deeper than it has ever been. You can experience your connection to the pivotal events and people in your life in a more profound way than ever before. That is what this book is about.

Part One

The Elements of Ritual

Opening to the Mystery

You have the wealth of the twenty-first century at your fingertips, yet there is a good chance that you feel impoverished and isolated. The magic of life and death, growth and mastery, loss and accumulation may elude you. Tied to your schedule, you stare at your computer for hours a day. You place your children in day care so you can work more, and you watch too much television because you are too tired to think.

The truth, though, is that you are a spiritual being who has chosen to have a human experience. Your soul deemed it necessary to experience life on earth, but when you are too busy to marvel at earthly miracles, you fail to feed your soul what it came to experience. The transition of summer to fall, the step from childhood to adulthood, the choice of whom to spend your life with, the move from one home to another—all these life transitions can be filled with satisfying experiences beyond words if you only had a way to honor them.

Your body comes from the earth. It is composed of the same clay and salt water that make up the land and the seas. The water in your body responds to the pull of the moon, just as the sea tides do. But you have forgotten this. Your body responds to the light and dark of the seasons as do the bodies of hibernating animals. Yet you usually do not notice. You have forgotten the deep joy of celebrating your earthiness. You have forgotten that when you leave one stage of life for the next, such as the step into parenthood or old age, changes happen at the physical, emotional, and spiritual levels. When you don't acknowledge and celebrate these changes, your life becomes less full than you deserve.

The act of ritualizing the events of your life allows the *inner* you to keep pace with the outer. Rituals take you to a place deeper than words. They satisfy in ways your spirit understands but your mind cannot.

A ritual is a conscious act that represents something deeper than the act itself. It can be as simple as deliberately experiencing the sunrise and knowing that, on this particular day, it means a whole new beginning for you. It can be as elaborate or humble as you choose.

The underlying significance of the ritual is its sacred meaning. The tangible expression of a truth that addresses the relationship between spiritual and physical experience will naturally reinforce your link to the sacred. The shift that happens in a powerful ritual moves you from ordinary space and time into a way of experiencing that which is formless and timeless. As you participate in a ritual, you may begin to understand such sacred principles as:

I am connected to all of life.

I am changing the course of my life now.

I am witness to the miracle that is happening.

I surrender to the changes that are occurring.

My blessings overflow.

Many of life's experiences are so profound that they are difficult to describe in words. These are the precise experiences you invite when you perform a ritual: you move yourself into change or unity, surrender or gratitude, in ways that are so powerful that they are beyond words. You experience true spirituality.

*T*hough not associated with any particular denomination or philosophy, the essential nature of ritual is sacred. The rituals in this book speak to the experiences that we all share just by being born on this earth. We share the seasons of the year and the seasons of our lives. Built into these cycles are sacred lessons that you are here to experience, lessons of unity, creation, change, and release. The sacredness of a ritual allows your spirit to inhabit these lessons in a way that goes deeper than words; that is the blessing of ritual.

It is also part of the mystery. By consciously participating in the physical world of form, you understand the truths of the spiritual world, that which is formless. For example, when you create a ceremony around the emergence of spring, fully experiencing the changing angle of the sun, the sprouting flowers, and the melody of the first birdsong, you come to experience your own immortality at a deeper level; that, too, is the blessing of ritual.

. *The Sacred Circle* .

*W*e begin with the circle, an ancient symbol of eternity. Life is full of circles and never-ending cycles. The circle of life generates birth, death, and rebirth, season after season. The sky above holds two circles, the moon and the sun. The blood in your body makes a circular journey from the heart through the body, and back through the heart again. Your very breath itself creates another circle as you breathe in through your nostrils, taking the nourishment into your lungs, and then breathe out through your mouth, expelling that which no longer serves the body.

The compass is a circular tool that displays the directions of the earth, each direction exerting its own energy and influence on us. A twenty-four hour day can be seen as circular; a project with a beginning, middle, and end is cyclical.

Many religions include the circle as a sacred symbol: the Hindu mandalas of India and Tibet, the medicine wheels of Native American culture, the Chinese yin-yang symbol, the Buddhist wheel of the eight-fold path, the Ouroboros (a symbol of a serpent or dragon forming a circle by biting its own tail and carrying the meaning of cyclic unity), and the wheel of the Zodiac, which bridges the energetic realm of symbolic animals and people and the literal world of form in the stars themselves.

The world's ancient cultures revered the circle as the sacred, cyclical symbol of the seasons, the life span, and the assurance of rebirth; it has always represented inclusion, oneness, and unity. (See the Wheel of the Year Calendar in Part Four.) Ancient people perceived the year as a cyclical period of time, as they did the life of an individual.

Conceptually, the circle, possessing neither beginning nor ending, is the opposite of a line, which contains both. The circle rotates, rolls and spins, having the movement of a line, yet always returning to where it began. The concept of "linear thinking," logically moving from one idea to the next to reach a conclusion, has a modern feeling to it, whereas "circular thinking" connotes a more ancient and organic way of looking at situations.

The circle and the line possess different characteristics. The circle feels complete, unified, secure, stable, continuous, and reassuring. By contrast, the line may feel uncertain and lonely, but adventurous and forever new. We do not know exactly where it is going nor where it will end up.

Our twenty-first century life holds much linear energy. "Progress" makes you feel you are going somewhere—exactly where you do not know, and more and more it can seem like a place you do not want to be. Even the way we read—in lines of letters and sentences—emphasizes linear living.

The unifying idea of rituals is the circle, appearing as it does in the cycle of the seasons and the seasons of your life.

Part Four of this book contains several "wheels" that illustrate the cyclic nature of life. Understanding and applying the relationship of the wheels to your life will give you more awareness of the circular energy in your life and that of the environment in which you live.

. *Using the Elements* .

*W*hen you learn how to incorporate the four sacred aspects of life—direction, element, energy, and symbol—into your rituals, you understand more clearly how the symbols of the earth harmonize with the various cycles of life. (See the Wheel of Activities in Part Four.) Notice that when you impose the Wheels over a compass, the mystical nature of the wheel becomes clear. The earth and its energies, symbols, and basic elements are in perfect harmony when seen on the sacred circle.

The direction in which we look to see the rising sun, east, is the direction of spring, new beginnings, and new ideas. The color associated with east is yellow, the color of the rising sun and of spring flowers. Yellow is also the color associated with mental clarity, and the east is the direction that carries the energy of mental clarity. When you have new ideas associated with new beginnings, you might say you are "inspired." Inspiration is literally breathing in God, and east is the direction associated with the element of air.

Using the Element of Earth

*E*arth is the element associated with the north, the part of the globe that holds most of the planet's landmass. Earth is the most solid, dense, and stable element.

Slow to change, durable in form, its energy is fixed, structured, and set in place. It is here to stay for a long time. The element of earth represents completion and endings. It is practical, results driven, and dependable. It is still. It is secure. It is also the source of our food, metals, flowers, trees, and even our physical bodies.

Earth represents material comforts and pleasures, so when we speak of someone as "earthy" we know them to be sensuous, practical, and "in their body." The earth element is closely related to our physical bodies, the chemical elements of which come from the earth. The minerals of the earth feed the solidness of our bones.

The earth element is evident in all that grows on the earth, thus representing the lavish abundance of earthly forms. All that the earth gives reminds us that we are secure, safe, and provided with the nourishment our bodies need.

The ancient alchemical symbol for earth is a triangle pointing downward with a horizontal bar through its center, depicting two layers of soil. Earth is a feminine element because it is from earth that new life emerges.

The symbolic colors of earth are white, the color of bones, and black, the color of fertile soil.

The ancient tool associated with this element is a pentacle, or five pointed star, which represents the stability and structure of this element.

You can use the earth element in ceremony when you want to call forth stability, structure, organization, or security. It can be used in rituals dedicated to the completion of a project or the celebration of an ending. The earth element in the form of a stone may be used to symbolize eternity or hard work. It may be used to symbolize nurturing or selfless generosity. When two stones are struck together—"click-click, click-click"—they simulate a heartbeat and can symbolize the giving or support of life. In the form of soil, the earth element may be used to symbolize the eternal self-givingness of life in support of new life. When a seed, a bean, or a bulb is planted in earth, both the seed and the soil can stand for the creation and manifestation of a desire. On the other hand, when we bury a symbol of something from which we wish to disengage, the earth will accept that thing we want to release and transmute it into nurturing energy.

Smooth stones have convenient surfaces to write upon, and writing an intention or blessing on a stone gives the words a feeling of being made solid in the life of the one who holds it. Contrast this weightiness with the feeling of writing a blessing or intention on a prayer flag and having the element of air blow the words and the intention all over the world.

Polished river rocks on an altar can simulate a beautiful river bed or path. The path, in turn, can symbolize one's path in life and can be made to diverge or come together, depending on the intent of the ritual.

The symbols associated with the earth element—the inverted banded triangle, the pentacle or star, the colors white and black—can be used in your rituals to suggest the symbolic meanings of their characteristics.

Using the Element of Air

Air, the invisible element in which we live and move, is associated with the east. We require this element in every minute of our earthly lives, and so it represents invisible support. It is the element of new ideas and intellectual ability. The word "inspire" means to breathe in the breath and ideas of God. Containing the energy of new beginnings, air is associated with mental skill, communication, logic, analysis, discernment, and decision.

Air is related to our sense of hearing since sound waves travel through the air. Communication with the spiritual realm belongs with this element. Prayers and chants are carried heavenward by the air. The smoke of peace pipes, the breezes blowing through prayer flags and carrying prayers around the world, and the dreams captured by dream catchers are transported by this element.

Air represents invisible change, like invisible winds affect visible forms.

The ancient alchemical symbol for air is a triangle pointing upward with a horizontal bar through its center, like a layer of clouds in the heavens above us. The upward pointing triangle is a phallic symbol and is associated with force and energy, especially that which is mental.

The color associated with air is yellow, the color of the sunrise, new beginnings, and mental clarity.

The ancient tool associated with air is the sword. It cuts through lies and confusion and symbolizes the attributes of learning, discernment, intelligence, conflict resolution, and communication.

You will use the element of air in a ritual when you wish to call forth inspiration, new beginnings, clear thinking, wise decision making, and vision. You will also use it when you want to send forth blessings, prayers, or support for change. Air is the invisible element, and so you will need to use ritual objects related to air that can be seen or held. Feathers, smoke, flags, scraps of material tied to a tree, chimes, bells, and voices all move through the air and can be used in your ceremony. An open book, its pages blown by the wind, symbolizes the wisdom that goes with inspiration and is an object that stands for the power of this element. The power inherent in air sends our prayers to places we cannot walk; it carries clarity to us from realms we cannot see; it spreads healing energy into the spaces too small for us to follow; it bears our burdens beyond our familiar world so that we can release them to the movement of the blessed wind.

Familiar sayings such as "the breath of life," "the winds of change," and "the bell of freedom" attest to the subconscious power of the invisible element of air.

The symbols associated with the air element—the upward pointing and banded triangle, the sword, and the color yellow—can be used in rituals to symbolize the characteristics of air.

Using the Element of Fire

*F*ire, the primal force that sets all creation in motion, is the element associated with south.

Beginning with what modern scientists call the "big bang," fire was at the forefront of our creation and still resides today as the molten core of the earth. Fire is the passion that sparks divine activity and moves us toward a goal. Fire is the sun; it is light; it is heat. It is the element that seems closest to the spiritual realm and furthest from earthly matter. Quick leaping flames with their ability to change fuel into ash represent instant transformation. Because of this, fire is associated with destruction, disappearance, or release. Conversely, the Hawaiian goddess of volcanoes, Pele, is associated with creation, as she creates new earth through her fire. A fire goddess from ancient Greece, Hestia, is associated with home, hearth, and warmth.

Fire symbolizes fervor, excitement, sexual passion, comfort, protection, courage, and enlightenment. The crucible, a container surrounded by fire in which all is that is not pure is burned away, symbolizes a test or challenge.

The ancient alchemical symbol for fire is a triangle pointing upward. This symbol reminds us of a leaping flame. A phallic symbol, it tells us that fire is a male element, with force and energy as its two major aspects.

The color associated with fire is red, the color of passion, anger, and heat.

Waving a red flag or cape at a bull causes him to charge in rage. Our own faces get red when we are angry or filled with passion.

The ancient tool associated with fire is the wand. Used in ritual to direct energy, it represents the yang characteristics of vigor, enterprising spirit, passion, power, and sexuality.

Fire is used in ceremony when you want to encourage dynamic activity, courage, energy for entrepreneurship, or passion for a love relationship. It can be used when you wish to increase the life force of a project or healing. To release something that is no longer wanted or needed, burn a symbol or a piece of paper on which the released thing or way of being is written. To illumine or inspire, light a candle in the darkness. Fire can be used to pass the warmth and unite a group in love, as in a Christmas candle-lighting ceremony; it can be used to announce the passion of an engagement, as in a sorority candle passing. Candles placed around the periphery of a room where a ceremony is taking place define the sacred space in which transformation happens. A lit candle can signify the spirit of a person who has passed on, just as the eternal flame burns at the grave of unknown soldiers. Dancing around a bonfire, leaping over a fire, and walking on smoldering coals are parts of rituals involving the high energy associated with deep, instant, and complete change.

The symbols associated with fire—the upward pointing triangle, the wand, the color red, hot coals, a candle, a spark, or lava rocks—can be used ceremoniously to inspire the high energy and transformative power of this element.

Using the Element of Water

*W*ater, the element that is most closely related to our human bodies, is associated with the west. Our bodies are 90 percent water, and it was from the vast oceans, covering 90 percent of the earth, that life emerged eons ago.

Water, the bloodstream of the earth, makes our lovely blue-green planet livable. Human bloodstreams hold almost exactly the chemical composition of the oceans. Water cleans the earth and our bodies. Therefore, in ritual, water can represent purification, nurturing, life-giving support, or creation.

Water in the forms of precipitation, oceans, lakes, rivers, wells, and springs, is necessary for human, animal, and plant life. In ancient times, natural wells and springs were holy sites. They represented thresholds between the dark, subterranean womb of earth and the bright, illumined surface. Water can represent the coming together of the conscious realms of thought and the subconscious beliefs and feelings deep within us.

Water is related to our feelings and emotions. Intuition, love, joy, peace, as well as sadness and fear, are feelings that transmit information and wisdom to our thinking processes. The waters of the earth are deep, as is the watery realm within us, telling us there is a connection between water and the subconscious mind and psychic powers.

Water also represents flexibility, nonresistance, and release. Flowing around obstacles, yet gradually wearing them down, water does not seek to master, but to relate, to cleanse, to accommodate.

The ancient alchemical symbol for water is a downward pointing triangle, the shape of the womb. Water is considered a feminine element and is related to emotions, nurturing, and love relationships.

The color associated with water is blue, the color of the deep seas that nurture the earth. Blue is also the color we call ourselves when we feel sad and needy.

The ancient tool associated with water is the chalice, symbolic of the womb, fluidity, intuition, emotional power, and love.

If you want deeper experience in love, if you have an area in your life that seems rigid and you want flexibility, if you want to develop your intuitive side, if cleansing, purification, revelation of the subconscious mind, or a symbolic rebirth is sought after, use water in your ritual. You can drink, sprinkle, or pour it. You may immerse yourself entirely; you may wash a part of your body or another's; you may bless yourself with a finger dipped in water. You may release symbolic items into running water or into the sea, thereby releasing the symbol's meaning from the life of the participant. Water from special healing wells may be brought to a ritual to bring the healing properties of that holy place.

Water and the symbols associated with water—the downward pointing triangle, the cup or chalice, the color blue—can be used in rituals to symbolize the characteristics of this element.

. *Creating Sacred Space* .

Creating a sacred space in which to perform your ritual will imbue the ceremony with greater emotional and spiritual weight. Through this act, you consciously form a place outside, or beyond, your everyday living space. You perform the ritual and then dismantle the space, returning life to normal.

Most rituals in this book are to be performed in a sacred circle. The Driver's License Ritual, the Ritual for Lovers, and the Maiden Ceremony, for example, call for the creation of a circle of flowers or petals as part of the ritual. Sacred circles can also be created with salt, cornmeal, or other objects appropriate to the ritual you are doing. The conscious creation of the circle itself, along with the agreement of the participants, establishes a dimension outside normal time and space in which extraordinary work can take place.

There is nothing particularly mysterious about creating sacred space. When a baby is born or when musicians improvise, they create sacred space. When actors, athletes, lovers, or even a group in deep conversation experience special insights or communion, they, too, create sacred space, whether consciously or unconsciously. In ritual, we create this space intentionally, anticipating an extraordinary experience.

The following technique for creating a sacred circle is called "calling in the directions." This ritual invites energy from the four directions of the compass to serve your endeavor. You may use this technique prior to any of the rituals in this book as a way to prepare the space and the participants for the ceremonies that will take place in the circle. You will require four candles: yellow, red, blue, and white.

✦

Calling in the Directions

*T*o begin the creation of your circle, invite all participants of the ritual to stand facing the East with their arms raised, palms out. The yellow candle is lit as the leader of the ritual begins.

Leader: "Welcome, East. We are open to your inspiration today. Give us your new ideas, new beginnings, new breath in our speaking. Let our view of today's endeavors be long, and let our seeing be expansive. Let this new day dawn in us with new and unlimited possibilities. Give us wisdom and insight for our work. Welcome, East."

Participants: "Blessed be" *(as in the goddess tradition), or* "Ho" *(as in the Native American tradition).*

Everyone turns to face the South while a red candle is lit.

Leader: "Welcome, South. May your heat live in our hearts as passion for our work together. May we feel the transformative power of your fire so that we are changed forever. May the bright energy of the sun illumine all that we do today. May we be surprised; may we laugh. Let your fire ignite our spirits. Welcome, South."

All respond, and then turn to the West. A blue candle is lit.

Leader: "Welcome, West. We are familiar with your watery ways because we are watery beings. Let our feelings have a place in today's work. May we regularly explore our mind and soul, not so much for answers as for questions. Let your way of intuitive certainty move in us for good today. Welcome, West."

All respond, and turn to face North while a white candle is lit.

Leader: "Welcome, North, the direction of the ancestors. May the wisdom of our relatives who have gone before influence our work today. May we be strong in body for what we are on this earth to do. Let it be that we do our work for those dear ones who will one day call us their ancestors. Welcome, North."

All respond.

Some traditions welcome only the four compass directions, while others invite three additional ones: above, below, and within. To continue the calling with these directions, the participants are now asked to look upward.

Leader: "Welcome, all the nations above. May the wisdom of the stars, planets, weather, and the wisdom of the beings that inhabit the sky be with us today. Let all your blessings fall on us and our work. May our ideas take flight as your energy enlivens us. Welcome, Above."

The participants respond, and then bend down to touch the earth.

Leader: "Welcome, Mother Earth. Let us feel our connection with you today. May our bodies of your clay find a comfortable home on you, and may your ways of flow, conservation, economy, support, and creation live in our work. Bless us, Mother Earth, and welcome."

All respond, then place their hands over hearts.

Leader: "We welcome the Great Within. May this inner universe that contains all we could ever need, be with us today. Let all that we are individually and collectively come forward and serve our work. Welcome to all that we are; welcome to the Great Within."

All respond.

Leader: "The sacred space has been established."

After the directions are called, the participants should feel prepared, divinely supported, full in the knowledge that the newly formed circle is a holy place in which powerful accomplishments are possible.

Closing the Directions

*W*hen the ritual is completed and the sacred circle is no longer necessary, it is meaningful for the directions to be closed and the space returned to its original state. This part of the "calling in the directions" reinforces the sanctity of the circle. The process goes backwards from the way the circle was created.

All participants stand with their hands over their hearts.

Leader: "We honor and thank the Great Within. All that was needed today was given and received. We have been fed, and the Great Within has been fed. Blessed be the Great Within."

Participants respond. Everyone bends down and touches the earth.

Leader: "Thank you, Great Mother, for enlivening us today. Thank you for your living creatures and your clay, both of which sustain us. May we harm nothing as we walk on your great body. Blessed be, Mother Earth."

All respond. All lean back their heads and face the sky.

Leader: "Thank you, Great Above, for watching over us and our endeavors today. May the heavens smile on us and continue to bless us all of our days at the bottom of your great sea of air. Blessed be, the Great Above."

All respond. All face North.

Leader: "Thank you, North, for being in service to us today. We see the grandmothers sitting in the north and smiling on us. May our bones be as strong as the mountains, and may our bodies be sustained to do the work we are here to accomplish. Blessed be, North."

All respond, and the white candle is extinguished. All face West.

Leader: "Thank you, West, for nourishing our intuition today. May you sustain our feeling nature in peacefulness, even though we take our leave from you now. May the salty waters of your seas move in our veins and keep us connected with you and with each other. Blessed be, West."

All respond, and the blue candle is extinguished. All face South.

Leader: "Thank you, South, for letting your passion live in us today. Power, transformation, spiritedness are your gifts, and we have accepted them. May your fire burn away all that is not in our best interest, leaving us pure and white hot to make positive changes in the world. Blessed be, South."

All respond, and the red candle is extinguished. All face East.

Leader: "Blessed East, thank you for reminding us that there is always another sunrise, always a new beginning. As we close this work and return our circle to normal time, space, and dimension, we honor you and give thanks that somewhere on this planet, our home, a new day is dawning and your energy is at work. May your newness have a receptive place in us. Blessed be, East."

All respond, and the final candle, the yellow one, is extinguished.

If the circle for the ritual has been created by flowers, salt, or another element, physically breaking the circle signifies the dissolution of the space that was created solely for the ritual. The leader can break the line of the circle by simply brushing away some of the petals or salt.

Leader: "The circle is broken, and our sacred work here complete. Blessed be."

Use of Symbols

A gold ring, a band without beginning or end, is a symbol of the endless love between two people. A doctoral certificate means that forever after this moment one will be addressed with the title "Doctor." But there are other symbols of life experiences that you may not have thought about before.

A stone or a piece of earth could represent the hours of service that you have given in the world.

A ball of yarn may be a symbol of connection. Wrapping a string of yarn around your wrist could signify that you are connected to something, either a person or an event, and the piece you carry after you break the yarn may remind you of this connection.

A flame might represent the passion in your heart. Lighting a candle, you may be reminded that the flame is eternal; it may be passed from candle to candle forever. So it is with your heart's passion and energy. Because passion and desire come from the Infinite, your own passion is forever available.

Using symbols that represent significant events or moments in our lives may deepen the experience of a ceremony or ritual. In the above examples, the stone, the yarn, and the flame represent service, connection, and passion. In another context or for another person, the symbols could mean something entirely different.

Conversely, the qualities of service, connection, and passion could be ascribed to completely different symbols. Depending on the goal of the ritual and the availability of objects, endless combinations of symbols and meanings are possible.

Grocery store produce departments, antique stores, craft and supply shops, your own attic or basement are great sources of symbols. When you have a ritual in mind that needs a symbol, wandering through these places with your mind wide open can be very productive.

The use of symbols in your ritual will deepen the experience because objects, being nonverbal, register in our hearts. Long after the ritual is finished, symbols carry meaning as they remind the participants of the original experience. The more powerful the ritual, the more the participants accept the deeper meaning of a symbol.

. *Ways to Release* .

Many rituals call for an element of releasing or letting go. This is important for rituals in which you wish to release an old way of being, such as when you leave a job, move from your home, dissolve a marriage, or say good-bye to something important to you.

Including an act of release into your ritual will more easily undo attachments that are particularly painful or difficult for you to let go of. On the other hand, if you are happy to be rid of a situation, the act of release can produce euphoria. In this case, the ritual integrates the absence of the old thing with your new way of being. A releasing ritual can also honor the end of an era or season, helping you remain conscious as you move and change in your life.

To understand where release and acceptance fit into the circle of life, refer to the Wheel of Activities in Part Four.

You can integrate the following actions into your rituals when you wish to release a particular person or experience:

Burn photos of that which you wish to release.

Write down on paper that which you wish to release, then burn the paper.

Stir a bowl of water counterclockwise.

Bury a symbol of that which you wish to release.

Blow out a candle.

Tear up, shred, untie, unbraid, or break a symbol of that which you wish to release.

Step through a doorway, over a threshold, or out of a circle.

Ways to Accept or Create

Many rituals acknowledge a new way of being which signifies that you are prepared to accept some specific object or condition in your experience, such as a relationship, wealth, peace, or inspiration. When you nurture the belief that the thing you want is able and willing to come to you, and that you are deserving of and prepared for it, no force will keep it away.

It is important that the object of your desire harms no one else. If you call forth conditions that are for the good of all and harm of none, you reinforce a worldview that life can work for everyone, not just a few. Conversely, if you call forth a condition in which you triumph over, dominate, or damage others, you reinforce a worldview in which harm is the norm. In that world, you are bound to be harmed sooner or later yourself, and you will have contributed to your own pain.

To accept or create something new in your life, incorporate the following practices into your rituals or celebrations:

Stir a bowl of water clockwise.

Fashion a symbol of your desire out of clay or dough.

Plant a symbol or a seed with your desire written on it.

Light a candle.

Braid or tie strands that symbolize the coming together of you with your desire.

Step over a threshold.

Write wishes on a gauzy piece of material, or create a dream catcher.

Attribute personal meaning to any symbol and keep it near you.

. *Altars* .

An altar is a physical site that has been designated as holy. It is a place where any-one may come to pray, meditate, ritualize, give thanks, receive blessing, or reflect on what is important and true. Although holiness is everywhere, there seems to be a palpable sense of the sacred at an altar. It can be a symbolic bridge between differ-ent worlds or states of being: between the spiritual world and the world of form, between the world of inner remembrance and outer awareness, between the state of confusion and the state of clarity.

In the great cathedrals and abbeys of Europe and the British Isles, the main altar is often built over the location of an earlier altar. That altar, in turn, is built on the same location where the pre-Christian temple altar stood before the church was built. Further, the temple altar would have been built directly over a sacred well that bubbled in prehistoric times. It is common for four or five churches and temples to have been built over the same location, one on top of the other, with the heart of the space, the altar, in the same spot throughout millennia.

The holy rituals that occurred on that spot—the appearance of the divine in a material form—although differing through the change of eras and belief struc-tures, must have been quite similar. While today it is the body and blood of Christ appearing through the bread and wine of Christian communion, back then it may have been an ear of corn in the Eleusinian mysteries celebrating immortality as taught by the goddess Demeter.

When you build your own altar, you assume that the same thing is happening; great holiness is revealed in your everyday life as blessing, clarity, connection, wisdom, inspiration, or spiritual support of some kind. Something important comes into your life from the world of possibility, and it is your altar that reminds you of this continuing miracle.

Altars are common in churches, but you may create one in your home, outdoors, or even in a hotel room. An altar can be the focal point of a ritual or just part of the decoration. It can be created for an evening or a lifetime.

An Advent Altar
(To celebrate the coming of the sun at winter solstice; the coming of the Son of God at Christmas)

*L*ong before Jesus' time on earth, the season of Advent (the four weeks leading up to Christmas) was a season of waiting. During this period the darkest time of the year was honored, the time when all living things and the earth itself waited for the return of the sun as promised by the winter solstice. For people who worked the soil, winter was the time to repair the farm equipment. Since turning the frozen soil would have been impossible during this time, they removed the wheels from their wagons and brought one wheel inside to decorate with evergreen boughs and red candles, symbolizing the green of the spring to come and the love of nature for her children.

You can build an Advent altar to honor the season of waiting by covering a table with gold, green, or red cloth and placing on it green boughs and red candles. On a wreath of dried vines or wood, place four red candles at the compass points of the directions.

On the first Sunday of Advent, light the first red candle and bring stones to your altar. Think and pray about the planet Earth and how you can take care of it. Contemplate the longing of the earth for the warmth of the sun; imagine how good the rays of the sun will feel in the coming spring. Speak the following:

One little candle lighted on the wreath.

The earth below prepares to glow.

On the second Sunday of Advent, light the second candle and relight the first. The second candle honors the plants of the earth. Bring greens, vegetables, fruit, nuts, winter berries and flowers to the altar to be added to the stones from the first week. Contemplate how we help the earth remain in balance, how essential the green plants are to the survival of all life on the planet. Recall how plants grow toward the sun and how, in their own way, they look forward to the increased light of the coming spring. Speak the following:

Two little candles lighted on the wreath.

A plant lifts up its blossom cup.

On the third Sunday, light three red candles and bring animals to the altar. Children may bring toy dinosaurs, photos of their pets, or a sheep or cow from their nativity set to bless this altar. Talk about how blessed we are to live with these wonderful animals. Contemplate how kindness to all living beings can be multiplied. Share about the excitement hibernating animals must feel when the sun lets them know that winter is over. Speak the following:

Three little candles lighted on the wreath.

The animals run to see the sun.

On the fourth Sunday of Advent, the Sunday before Christmas, light all four red candles to honor the human beings of the earth. Figurines and photos are appropriate to add to the altar. This is a time to recognize that all the people of the earth belong to one spiritual family. Contemplate peace, sharing, connection, all the qualities that are needed to live together in harmony. Share about how the light on the outside reminds us of the light on the inside. Speak the following:

Four little candles lighted on the wreath.

The people's sight is washed by light.

On Christmas Eve, a few days after the winter solstice, light all four red candles and add a white candle in the center of the wreath. Next to the candle, place a figurine of a baby or the baby Jesus from your nativity set. Contemplate how the light of the Creator has lit the path of spiritual seekers of all traditions in every era, and that the light is always available to us. Speak the following:

> *One white candle lighted in the wreath.*
> *A baby is born to warm the earth, to fill our cup, to lift us up.*

A First Harvest Altar
(To appreciate your limitless blessings and show gratitude)

*I*n ancient times, the harvest celebration began around the beginning of August when the fruit and vegetables were ripest. This is a perfect time of year to create an altar of bounty and to use it to remind yourself of that which you appreciate in life yet take for granted.

Go to the market and purchase red apples and radishes, oranges and carrots, yellow squash and lemons, and on through the rainbow, ending with a trail of purple grapes. Cover a table with a beautiful cloth and arrange the produce on the altar with a bouquet of celery stems and broccoli heads in the center. This is a wonderful opportunity to share the bounty at a dinner party with family or friends. Offer your guests the contents of the altar to take home, blessing their next meal with the love that was shared during the time together around the First Harvest altar.

The produce can also be arranged as though the fruits and vegetables are pouring out of a cornucopia, or horn of plenty. Although it is more traditional to use this symbol closer to Thanksgiving, with Indian corn, winter squashes, nuts, and pumpkins pouring out, it will work with earlier crops just as well.

The origin of the horn of plenty has its roots in the prehistoric past. In some cultures the Horned God, central to many ancient pantheons, was a deity with the body of a man and the antlers of a stag or horns of a ram; in other cultures he was a creature with small horns and cloven hooves. Called Pan in ancient Greek culture, he was the god of wine, hedonism, and inspiration. Known as Cernunnos in the Celtic culture, he was the god of animals, fertility, and abundance. The story goes that Cernunnos broke off one of his horns and poured from it never ending blessings to the people of earth. Later, Christians transformed this horned one's image into that of the devil.

An Altar to Bless Loved Ones, Talismans, and Crafts

*A*t an annual women's retreat, I once created a communal altar out of a large table with two shelves placed on top. We began with an acknowledgment that we were creating sacred space together. We further agreed that the items placed on the altar would bless all other items, and that each item will be blessed by the combined energy of all the items.

First we placed photos of people precious to us on the altar, along with personal objects of deep meaning. As the week progressed, the sacred space expanded as we added various crafts we had made. Throughout the retreat, many participants spent quiet time at the altar, contemplating the love, the pain, the openness, the creativity, the inspiration, and the connection represented by the objects on the altar. At the end of the retreat, the objects had become sacred reminders of our great leaps in understanding and wisdom.

Placing familiar items on a personal home altar, a space that you have designated as "holy," will remind you daily of the meaning and inspiration of the objects.

An Altar to Request a Blessing or an Answer

*A*t home I have a statue of an angel holding half a clam shell like a shallow basket in her hands. The shell is about an inch and a half across, just the right size to hold a small piece of paper with a request written on it. I often include the angel in my personal altar at home, along with candles, flowers, and colors that are seasonally or energetically symbolic to me. In the clam shell, I place my prayer requests for a particular condition or answer. Writing my request helps me become clear about what I am ready to receive in my life. The ritual is meaningful to me, and I have found that writing out requests and offering them in a symbolic way is meaningful to others, regardless of age or spiritual belief.

Any kind of receptacle in which to place requests can be a wonderful addition to your altar. In some honorable and ceremonial way, with reference to a deity or to life in general, place your request in the receptacle and wait for your answer or blessing.

The creation of a sacred box or the decoration of a basket or bowl for prayer requests can be a great project for a family or group, as is the creation of the altar on which to place it.

An Altar for a Ritual of Inclusion or Membership

A church or organization could create a special altar for a new member ritual. Place a green or brown cloth on a large table. On it, build a winding path of smooth river stones, each stone approximately one inch in diameter, representing a stream or riverbed. You can bunch up small pillows or plastic bags underneath the cloth to simulate hills in the landscape, around which you can add candles, potted plants, or vases of flowers. This altar symbolizes the common path of all who are a part of the group or organization.

Before the ritual begins, each new member is given a stone. After being asked to contemplate what quality they will bring to the group, the new members write this quality on their stone with a metallic marker. As they hold the stone to their heart, they vow to bless themselves and the group by giving this quality. Placing their stone in the riverbed, they become united with the group as a whole.

At each subsequent new member induction, the stones from the previous years can be placed in the riverbed as the altar is built, symbolizing the gifts that members have brought over the years and allowing new members to see that their gifts join the gifts of others who have come before them, preparing their way into the organization.

Altars Honoring the Directions

*W*hen you understand the flow of a year, the activities associated with each direction make sense and feel comfortable. (Refer to the Wheel of Directions, Elements, Energies, and Colors in Part Four.) You can make an altar for each direction and celebrate the energies called through the East, South, West, and North. Or you might incorporate elements for each direction into a single altar. If four altars are created, one for each direction, participants can find their way to the appropriate altar for the energy they are seeking at that time. Or a ritual could be created so the gifts from all directions may be received.

Another application of the gifts of the directions is to make four altars and sit inside the circle they create, experiencing the energies as they flow to you from each direction. Posing a question about a decision you need to make and feeling the wisdom flowing to you from each direction can be a powerful solitary practice.

The following are suggestions for creating altars honoring the directions.

Altar in the East

Create this altar using yellows and other bright spring colors. East represents new beginnings, inspiration, and new thoughts. The element of air is celebrated here. This is the direction of youth and is representative of the self-reliance of a teenager setting out on his or her life path with an "I can do it myself" attitude. Symbols for this altar include feathers, streamers, and flags waving in the air. Bells celebrate the East as their ringing vibrations travel through the air. Directions for spiritual work done at the eastern altar might include:

Welcome to the East.

Celebrate new beginnings.

Be inspired and breathe deeply.

Heal limited thoughts.

Altar in the South

Use reds, oranges, and other hot, fiery colors for this altar. South is the direction of love, passion, creativity, family, and high energy. It is the direction symbolizing a mother's love for her baby, as well as the passion of lovers. The red of the South represents blood, fire, life force, and transformation. Symbols for a southern altar may include a candle's flame, charred pieces of wood, hearts, a cauldron, or burning bowl. Directions for spiritual work done at the southern altar might be:

Welcome to the South.

Live your passion.

Heal low energy.

Step into the fire.

Altar in the West

Dark blues, purples, and indigoes are appropriate for the western altar, the direction and color of the setting sun. This direction invites you to turn within, as the autumn season invites you inside your home. This is the direction of completion and the deep satisfaction that comes with the end of a job well done. West is also the direction of our emotions; troubling, joyful, and those that fall in-between. It represents the era of your life when you turn from adult to elder. Symbols for a western altar include a goblet of water and other items that one would find in the sea, such as shells and coral. Directions for spiritual work in the west could include:

Welcome to the West.

Turn within.

Feel it and heal it.

Give thanks for blessings and completions.

Altar in the North

The northern altar does not include much color, just as the far North lacks variety of color; everything is black and white. This is the direction of the mystery of death and rebirth. It is where the "old hag" dies and becomes the infant, where Father Time with his sickle of death transforms into the New Year's baby. It is the direction of our ancestors and the white bones that remain after the spirit has left the body for another experience. The element of north is earth. Symbols for the altar in the North include stones, bones, and the yin-yang with the point of light emerging in the field of darkness. Directions for spiritual work in the North might be:

Welcome to the North.

Celebrate the mystery of death and rebirth.

Heal your body and the earth.

Transform and become new again.

Part Two

The Seasons of the Year

. Seasonal Celebrations .

*W*e celebrate annual holidays with traditions often begun by parents or grandparents who received the traditions from their ancestors. We unquestioningly associate cultural symbols with our holidays, such as eggs at Easter or baskets of flowers on May Day, without knowing why. Yet if we understood the roots of these symbols and holidays, we could make the celebrations much more meaningful.

When the significance of a celebration becomes diluted as we forget the original reason for the tradition, rituals can help create new traditions filled with depth, meaning, and gratitude. Rituals can make our seasonal holidays truly holy, helping us understand our connection with life as we celebrate the special days that come around year after year.

This section gives some brief history of ancient holidays and their modern manifestations. It is helpful to refer to the Wheel of the Year Calendar in Part Four as you read on.

*S*easonal holidays marked the cycle of the year for our ancestors. Every aspect of the seasons—the weather, the natural growth cycle of plants, animals, and humans, the amount and angle of the sunlight, and the timing of sunrise and sunset—was part of the holy turn of the year. The cycle of planting and harvesting crops was not only essential work for ancient people, it was holy work. Harsh winters necessitated staying indoors, reminding ancient people that the inner world is as important as the outer. When you incorporate some of these ancient values and traditions into your modern day celebrations, you ease the alienation from the natural cycle of life.

Today we are more estranged from the earth and its cycles than ever before. Consider how our culture denies the naturalness and the value of aging, as seen by the cosmetic industry, plastic surgery, hormone therapy, ageist hiring practices, and the treatment of the elderly. Most of us are uncomfortable with the idea of growing old.

Also lost to our culture is the organic nature of eating food indigenous to particular places and times of the year, as well as the appreciation of experiencing the seasons as they naturally occur. We think nothing of shipping fresh food over vast distances so that "out of season" produce will always be available. We treat seasonal depression as a disorder rather than accept that we simply act differently in the winter as we become more interior and quieter than we are in the summer.

You can celebrate the holidays of your ancestors through rituals. Some of these ancient holidays have evolved into familiar celebrations, such as Christmas, Easter, and Halloween. The ancient northern European celebrations that correspond to these three modern holidays are Yule, Ostara, and Samhain, words often associated with "pagan" rites.

"Pagan" refers to "any religion that is not derived from Judaism, Christianity, or

Islam." Although that definition sounds rather benign, many of us negatively connote the concept of paganism with ideas such as "fertility cult," "barbarian," "idolatry," and "devil worship." Yet pagan spirituality is the historic source of every modern religion. The alienation from our historic roots arose out of religious fear and the necessity to believe that the religious doctrines in current practice are "right" and any others are "wrong."

"Pagan" originally referred to "a country person," someone who lived away from towns. From ancient times to the present, people who think of themselves as pagans see spirituality in nature rather than in a book or in a building, or even in a particular person or deity. Pagans experience holiness in the four basic elements: earth, air, fire, and water. They see the divine in all aspects of the natural world, including the change of the seasons and the cycles of their own lives. They celebrate the naturalness of this earthly life in growth, maturation, and aging, in birth and death, in light and dark, in the growing cycle of crops, and the changing weather. Seeking the experience of connection with the divine source has been the desire of every spiritual artisan through the ages, no matter what designation of religious group. Desire for divine connection operated in our pagan ancestors as it today operates in modern pagans, just as it is operating in those who practice a spiritual path of any organized religion or one of their own making.

Whether you consider yourself a pagan, a member of any modern denomination, or not religious at all, the seasonal rituals and celebrations in this book will bring you closer to the deep joy of participating with the sacred seasons of earth.

. *Wheel of the Year* .

*T*oday we picture the year as a document of twelve pages, each page of which is torn off and discarded as the months pass. Ancient people, though, experienced the year circularly, season following season. The seasonal circle has no "beginning," unlike today when we say the year begins with the month of January. The constant turning of the seasons was, to them, an endless wheel of changing light, precipitation, temperature, and energy within the unchanging uniformity of the cycle of life. It was a secure structure for our ancestors, year in and year out.

Human cultures the world over have based their life and their spirituality on the cycle of the seasons. In this book, I follow the seasons in the northern hemisphere of the earth, while being aware that the seasonal changes in the southern hemisphere form the yearly structure for indigenous people in that part of the world.

The circular year is represented with winter at the top of the circle, also thought of as North, with spring to the right or East, summer at the bottom or South, and autumn to the West or on the left side. (Follow along on the Wheel of the Year and Wheel of the Year Calendar in Part Four.) For our purposes, we'll enter the circle at the top, although we could enter it at any point because there really is no beginning or end to the cycle.

Winter Solstice—Yule

*A*t the top of the circle of the year, the world is dark, cold, and quiet, with short days and long nights. The fields and forests are dormant, with much of the land on the northern half of the planet covered with snow. For many weeks, the days have been shorter than the nights, and the level of activity for humans and animals has decreased with many furry creatures in hibernation and humankind sheltered indoors. For six months prior, the amount of darkness has been increasing each day and the sunlight decreasing.

Then, in the magic of an instant, light is reborn. The winter solstice occurs the moment the amount of daily darkness begins to decrease. For the next six months, the amount of daily light will increase until the moment at the opposite side of the circle when, once again, the darkness begins overtaking the light.

The magic of the winter solstice is the rebirth of life at the time of greatest darkness. It reminds us that new life, whether deep in the soil or deep in a womb, begins in the darkness as a secret. The announcement of new life, whether as a sprout or as the birth of a young one, is still a ways off. Germination, conception, and the moment of the winter solstice each promise a new life and is, therefore, sacred.

Ancient people called the holiday of the winter solstice *Yule,* a word that continues today as a part of our Christmas tradition. At Yule our forefathers and mothers celebrated the birth of the sun; Christmas celebrates the birth of the Son. Both holy days bring the promise of renewal and new beginnings. The light born out of the darkness is both the ancient and contemporary message of this holiday.

Ground Hog's Day—Imbolc

*T*he quarter holidays of the ancient calendar correspond to the means and the extremes of the sun's journey across the sky, occurring on the shortest day, the longest day, and the two days of the year when the day and night are of equal length. There are also holidays in between the quarter holidays called cross-quarter holidays. Taken together, the year consists of eight major holidays falling about six weeks apart. (See Wheel of the Year Calendar in Part Four.)

Following the winter solstice, as the sun begins to show itself for a few minutes more each day, the next holiday occurs on February 2. *Imbolc* literally means *ewe's milk* and occurred during the time of year when the new lambs were born. It was a holiday of increased light but not yet increased temperature. Winter continues in the northern hemisphere in early February, yet the promise of the spring cannot be denied. During this holiday, ancient people blessed the seeds which were to be planted as soon as the land thawed. The tools of their trades were cleaned, blessed, and re-consecrated to the tasks they would accomplish once winter ended.

The remnants of Imbolc have turned into Ground Hog's Day. On this day, if the ground hog sees its shadow when it pokes its nose out of its burrow, there will be six more weeks of winter. If the skies are cloudy with no shadows cast, however, spring is just around the corner. This may seem backwards, but a look into the pagan roots of this holiday shed light on this logic.

In Celtic lands, which reached from the British Isles across Northern Europe, lived Brigit, the goddess of Imbolc (later transformed into St. Brigid by the Catholic church). When spring approached, Brigit appeared on the land, admiring the beauty of late winter and blessing the first little green sprouts about to emerge through the crusty, melting snow. If spring were near, Brigit would be smiling down at the ground hog as he came up, casting her long shadow over his. His shadow obscured by Brigit's, the ground hog knew that spring was almost ready to burst forth. However if spring was far off, Brigit would not yet be strolling over the earth, and the ground hog would see his shadow.

Spring Equinox—Ostara

*T*he next solar holiday occurs when the day and night are in perfect balance—the spring equinox. Ancient Europeans called this holiday *Ostara* in honor of the Germanic goddess Eostre, the same word that gave us "Easter" (and "estrogen!"). By the end of March, spring is in full swing; trees and meadows are in bloom; warmth has returned to the land, and the earth is running in fertile muddy streams from the melting snow and spring showers. The symbols of Eostre were rabbits and eggs because they represent the essence of fertility; spring is riotous in her affirmation of abundant new life. Hillsides aflame in wildflowers, bees buzzing around white, pink, and yellow trees tell us that Eostre still blesses earth at this time of year.

Spring is the time of planting. As soon as the land was able to be tilled, the seeds that were blessed at Imbolc were planted in the dark, fertile mud of the earth. This celebrated a time in which the people affirmed, year after year and century after century, that life emerges once again from apparent death. The people worked with that cycle in the planting of the crops that would carry them through the next winter, still far away but promised.

The most holy of Christian holidays is fashioned after this ancient, earthy celebration. Easter was transformed into a lunar holiday because it is always the first Sunday after the first full moon after the spring equinox. No matter your religion, the magic of new beginnings becomes evident in this season with its symbols of bunnies, eggs, flowers, and new life. We feel a new "lease on life," another chance; anyone suffering from the seasonal depression of winter darkness feels the gloom lifting. This enlivening feeling seems to come upon us as a gift, and the prehistoric doubt that spring might not come again disappears along with the frost of last winter. We are born again!

May Day—Beltane

As we spin ourselves around the wheel of the year, the light, heat, and life energy all build; we are approaching the hot time of year, both in air temperature and energy. On May 1st, we come to an ancient holiday called *Beltane*. The word *Beltane* means "bright fire," and to our ancestors this was a holy day of fire within and without. Sexual passion and lust, celebrated by ancient people at Beltane, kindle controversy in our culture today. For many of us, sex does not fall on the sacred end of the spectrum; the pleasure of sex seems to be physical, not mystical. We receive mixed messages about our sexual expression from society. We are usually not taught that our bodies are sacred, nor that sexual pleasure can be a form of worship.

Yet the inviolability of our bodies and the naturalness of sexual activity, characteristic to this time of year for ancient people, manages to seep into our culture in subliminal ways. In the Disney classic *Bambi*, young Bambi, Thumper, and Flower find themselves "twitterpated." The Broadway musical *Camelot* refers to "The Lusty Month of May." Like our ancestors, we know that late spring is a wonderful time to "go a-Maying."

The symbols of Beltane were the maypole and flower baskets. If you ever danced around a maypole or placed flower baskets on your neighbors' doorstep on May Day, you were actually honoring male and female sexual parts and the actual act of sexual intercourse as represented by the colorful ribbons wrapping around the maypole.

The month of May is named for the Roman goddess Maia, who was honored with a garland of flowers carried through the town on top of a long pole. Although this May holiday evolved with contributions from Greek, Roman, Celtic, and other cultures, the theme of fertility, life force, sexual, and creative passion remained constant. In Celtic lands the Green Man, a symbol of nature, became the consort of the Queen of the May in order to ensure a good crop. In some places a man and woman from the village enacted the roles of the Green Man and the Queen of the May, celebrating sexually in sacred ritual for the benefit of the entire town. In some places great bonfires were built, and the cattle were driven between the fires to ensure protection and fertility for the coming year. In others, couples celebrated by leaping over the bonfires and then making love in the forest.

Today, the original meaning of the maypole is lost to us. There is something healthy and holy about celebrating and giving thanks for one of the greatest physical pleasures available to us.

Summer Solstice—Litha

The next holy day, *Litha*, is halfway around the calendar from where we started. The summer solstice occurs when the germ of darkness in the midst of the greatest light begins to grow; the longest day gives way to the half of the year in which the darkness grows and grows until, once again, at the winter solstice the light begins to increase.

Midsummer, or Litha, celebrates the most vibrant time of expression in nature. The sun is at its zenith, emanating more heat and light to the northern hemisphere. The trees are at their fullest, the growth rate is fastest, and the activity level at this time is the highest. In some towns and villages in the northern hemisphere the sky never gets totally dark at Midsummer, but maintains a grayish light throughout the night. Given their own body rhythm, people stay awake and active longer at Midsummer; the light and warmth allow many northern people to play summer sports long into the night. It is natural for us to be more active in the summer, as it is natural for us to be more inactive in the winter when it is cold and dark.

In addition to heightened activity levels, there are other energies that have been associated with this time of year through the ages, but are largely forgotten in our modern culture. Committed love, trickery, and fairies all play important roles in Midsummer. As Beltane was the holiday of wild, passionate sexual play, Midsummer takes that wild expression and turns it into the love of committed relationship. Perhaps with new life imminent after conception, the commitment to family life seems natural. Whatever the evolution, it has come down to us in modern times that June is "wedding month." To be a June bride is special; it seems like a natural time to commit to lifelong love.

The aspects of trickery, playfulness, and surprise come with this time of year. It is said that the veil between the fairy kingdom and the human world is especially thin at Midsummer. Fairies are free to play their games of mischief on humans at this time of the cycle, and in Celtic lands fairies and humans form long hand-to-hand chains and dance through villages to bonfires built on hilltops, singing and celebrating the long dusk of Midsummer.

Superimposing the Native American medicine wheel on the European wheel of the year, we find the coyote in the position of South, or Midsummer. The shamanic coyote, known as the trickster, is responsible for much mischief done in the human realm.

Shakespeare's play *A Midsummer Night's Dream* plays with this season's themes of committed love, trickery, and fairies. The character Puck plays mischief on the human and fairy realms, alike. He is the messenger of the Fairy King Oberon who plays a nasty trick on his wife, Queen Titania, causing her to fall in love with a simple human craftsman with an ass's head. The play ends with a glorious celebration of three weddings. Puck's closing line of this "dream" in which reality and the insubstantial realms constantly commingle is "Lord, what fools these mortals be." It is the perfect message for this mischief-ridden play and the holiday it depicts.

Early Autumn—Lughnasa

*A*s the days begin to shorten from the moment of Midsummer, the next cross-quarter holiday approaches with the autumn. Although the days remain warm, the tree branches begin turning orange in anticipation of the full fall color that is to arrive. *Lammas* was originally called *Lughnasa* (pronounced "LOO-nuh-suh), in honor of the Celtic deity and hero Lugh. The Christianized word "Lammas" means "loaf-mass," and this holiday celebrates the first cutting of the grain for the year.

Although no modern holiday corresponds to this ancient celebration, its festive energy continues to impress itself on us. Today most state and county fairs are scheduled in the month of August; these are social celebrations of our modern harvests. At farmers' markets in autumn, corn and other grains, watery vegetables such as summer squashes and peppers, berries, stone fruit and grapes appear in abundance. The traditional school year, beginning in late August or September, was also established in ancient times to allow young people to help with the harvest before they began their studies.

Throughout the past, food has played an essential part in worship. The planting, tending, and harvesting of food was considered as sacred. Halfway back through the year, at Imbolc, the seeds of the crops were blessed. At the spring equinox they were planted. In the hot, light part of the cycle they were tended. At harvest time the sacrifice of the grain was celebrated. The cycle symbolizes the principle that life supports life; our soul cannot remain in our bodies unless we consume other life-forms, whether they be plant, animal, or both. For ancient people, the life of the grain was as important as any other life, even more so because grain has always been know as the "staff of life." The first cut of the grain and the first loaf of bread made from that grain was a part of the celebration of this holy day.

The wine made from the first grapes of the harvest at Lammas was also considered sacred. When the body of the deity was sacrificed at this celebration, the bread represented his body and the wine, his blood. The consumption of the holy body and holy blood was done in thanksgiving and in order to absorb the spirit of the Holy One in sacred ceremony. This ancient custom remains with us today as the Christian church's communion.

Autumn Equinox—Mabon

*T*he autumnal equinox (*Mabon* in ancient times) is the second day of balance in our yearly cycle, the second time in the year when the day and night are of the same length. The crops from this time of year are the heavier, starchy vegetables that nourished ancient people through the cold months: winter squashes, potatoes, star fruits, apples and pears, and the sensuous pomegranate.

As the temperature drops and the darkness comes earlier, humankind feels the need to slow down and take stock of what has been cultivated through the year. The time of gratitude is here. It is a time to look back and review our lives, realizing that the seeds planted in spring have grown into the crop of our lives. After the harvest, ancient peoples returned the farming tools to the barn. They used this time of year to can, smoke, and dry the food they would need for the winter. Activity moved from outdoors to indoors, just as our energy wants to move to the interior world. As with the sun, we experience this time of balance as a good time to give thanks for all the blessings of life.

Halloween—Samhain

*T*he darkness becomes greater than the light as the calendar moves into the last quarter of the year. However, the ancient world did not see darkness as evil, as our modern world often does, obsessed as it is with light, spring, and youth. For them, the darkness represented the womb of life, the source of intuition, the balance in opposition to the light, the divine mystery, the doorway between the worlds.

The last cross-quarter holiday is *Samhain* (pronounced "SOW-in"), holiday of death and remembrance. Samhain looks across the circle at Beltane. From this point of view, we are aware of two aspects of modern life that are troublesome for us— sex and death; these polar aspects of life were equivalent in sacredness with the growing cycle for ancient peoples. Conception, birth, planting, cultivating, sexual desire, mating, eating, maturing, reaping, resting, and dying were all gifts from the realms of Holy Ones to the children of earth.

Samhain was the holiest night of the ancient year, the time when the veil between the physical and spiritual worlds was thinnest. It was believed that communication with our departed family members was possible on this night. It has come down to us today as Halloween, with many of the ancient symbols still intact—jack-o-lanterns to show the departed souls the way back to their earthly homes, the favorite foods of the dead set out for when they came visiting from the realm beyond, costumes worn as disguises to hide from one's ancestors.

Samhain was also the harvest of the animals. This was the time when animals were blessed and asked to give their bodies for food so that our bodies might be sustained through the winter.

After Samhain, life in the northern hemisphere becomes dormant. The earth rests beneath gray skies and a low sun, and burrowing animals stay snug in their underground homes. In winter ancient people spent time indoors mending their clothing, repairing their farming tools, telling stories, and sleeping. However, we do not slow down much in winter today. With the holiday time of the year upon us in November and December, we have more and more to do, giving ourselves the illusion that winter is just like summer, only colder.

The circle has been spun; the next holiday is where we began. The sun is reborn once again, and the blessed cycle keeps on spinning with half the year moving to increased light, heat, and activity and half the year moving to darkness, cold, and rest. Half of the year is for youth; half of the year is for maturity. Half of the year is for outward movement; half of the year is for inward movement. Death is as sacred as birth; and the old have their beauty as do the young. The buds are as sacred as the falling leaves. Balance is the overarching gift of earthly life bringing all of our blessings together as in this ancient chant:

Lady, spin your circle bright.
Weave your web of dark and light.
Earth, air, fire, and water
Bind us as one.

As you celebrate the rituals of the seasons, refer to the Wheel diagrams in Part Four. As you observe the position of the holiday on the wheel, see what corresponds to the same position of the other wheels.

. *Winter Solstice Ritual* .

The Winter Solstice Ritual, which welcomes the energy of the returning sun, can be celebrated with a group or by yourself by simply using the leader's comments as the direction for your own contemplation and responses. A couple could celebrate this ritual by alternately reading the words of the leader and doing the activities together.

Materials:

    Fire bowl—a container for holding burning pieces of paper

    Paper—use flash paper if possible, found in magic stores

    A pen or pencil for each person

    One large white candle

    One smaller white candle in a glass holder for each person

    One metallic pen for each person

    Shamanic flute music

Set up:

    Create an altar in the middle of the room with all candles, unlit, arranged on the altar, the large one in the center of the smaller ones. Place the fire bowl on the altar. Decorate the altar with special stones, animal bones, or pieces of fur. Arrange chairs in a circle around the altar, one for each participant including the leader. The participants enter, take a writing instrument and paper, and sit in the circle of chairs. The lighting should be low.

⚛

Leader: "We are here to consider the mystery of transformation, of death and rebirth, of light emerging from the darkness, of the new emerging from the ashes of the old. We are here to honor this mystery in our world and in ourselves, for as it is in the great whole, so it is in the individual. Are you all ready to do your part in this transformation so that the great mystery of rebirth may prove itself once again in you?"

Participants: "We are."

Leader: "As we come to the end of the great darkness for this cycle of our world as it spins around the sun—our source of light and heat—we leave anything we would like to release or let go of in the darkness. Take the paper and writing instrument in your hands, and let your awareness fall deep within you. As you review this last year with its seeds of possibilities, the work and dedication you have given to your life and activities, all that has been given to you in the way of harvest, ask yourself, 'What are those things that feel complete? What are those things that have withered of their own accord yet continue to take up space in your thoughts or in your heart; those people or relationships that are ready to be finished in the way that they have been; projects, dreams, concerns, wars, disappointments, accomplishments, ways of being that no longer serve you?' Now write down a list of words or symbols that represent each and every thing that you are ready to release."

The participants write.

Leader: "Look over this list. As we move further into this ritual there will come a moment when the darkness takes these things from you, moving them into a state of nothingness, and they will no longer be in your life to use up your energy. Carefully reflect on the things that have given their gifts to you and are now complete, for they will be gone."

Pause.

Leader: "Are you ready to release those things that no longer serve you?"

Participants: "We are."

Leader: "As you come forward, place your paper in the fire bowl and chant with me, 'Purify and heal me. Heal me and free me.'"

The participants come forward placing their papers in the fire bowl, repeating the chant until all have come forward.

Leader: "As I light these papers symbolizing all that you are ready to release, know with me that the darkness—the blessed, fertile darkness—generously takes all that is complete in our lives. It takes it with no harm to itself or any living being. It takes it and transforms it into potentialities and possibilities for other people in other times and places to create events, relationships, and circumstances in their lives that bless and teach them. As the flames consume these papers, know with me that all these events, projects, conditions, and ways of being are truly dissolved and gone from your life."

Leader lights the papers and burns them in the bowl.

Leader: "You are now as empty as a flute with no melody, as clear as a mirror with nothing reflected, completely in the field of pure potentiality. As the following music is played, feel yourself as empty as a furrow in the field before the seed is planted, as empty as a page before a thought is written."

Play several minutes of shamanic flute music. Lights should be turned off completely. Several minutes of silence follow the flute music, and then play the music for a few more minutes. The leader prepares to light the large candle in the center of the altar.

Leader: "The rebirth is almost at hand; the light in the darkness is ready to be reignited—the transformation of that which was into that which will be is about to happen."

Leader lights the large candle.

Leader: "Lighting this candle symbolizes that which is now taking place, physically and spiritually, in hearts and minds the world over. We celebrate it here together. Let your eyes open softly to witness the light from within the darkness. This light burns in you and through you. There is a place for you to shine your light this coming year. In this moment let that place come to you. It may be a project that will change the lives of millions of people, or it may be the healing that comes with one act of compassion; it may be a single piece of what you will do this year, or it may be the entire work. What is it that the light wants to be in you this year? Come forward now. Take a candle, light it, and write on the glass holding the candle, in words or symbols, what the light wants to be in you this year."

Participants come forward, take a smaller candle, light it from the larger candle, and write their message on the glass with the metallic pens.

Leader: "With your candle in your hands, share with one other person what your light will be this year, and then replace your candle on the altar."

Participants mingle and share the message of their light and then return their candles to the altar. The only light in the room is from the candles.

Leader: "See how brightly the sacred light shines. The light has once again been born from the darkness. The old has left us, and the new is shining from within us. Just as one candle flame could light a candle held by every person on this planet, may the light in this room go forth to heal and bless the whole world. Join me in saying, 'Bless the light.'"

All: "Bless the light!"

. *Late Winter Ritual* .

The Late Winter Ritual plants intentions for the imminent growing season by creating a garden of light. It also rededicates the instruments of your work. Ritualizing the ancient celebration of Imbolc, when the days are noticeably longer and the promise of a new spring is in the air, it is an ideal time to create clear intentions. Though written for a group of celebrants, a single person could perform this ritual by reading the leader's words and following the directions.

Materials:

    Small pieces of pale green paper

    Writing instruments for each person

    One small garden pot filled with potting soil for each person

    Bowl of alyssum seeds

    One four-inch taper candle for each person

    Altar

    One copy of "self blessing," rolled up and tied, for each person

    Matches

Preparation:

    Invite all participants to bring a symbol of the work to which they are dedicating their life. For example, a student could bring a notebook and pencil; a doctor could bring a stethoscope; a businessperson could bring a business card.

Set up:

Create an altar that includes the garden pots filled with potting soil. Place an unlit candle in each pot to symbolize a growing sprout. Place the bowl of seeds, the stack of green papers, the writing instruments, and the rolled "self blessings" on the altar.

ϕ

Leader: "Welcome to the late winter time of the yearly cycle. This is the time of increased light, but not yet increased heat. Today we will dedicate ourselves to the work of the year and sanctify the tools of our work and ourselves."

Pass out the following items to each person or have a helper distribute them: the pot with the soil and candle, the green paper, a writing instrument.

Leader: "There is work that wants to be accomplished through you. When we dedicate ourselves to the work that is ours to do, the universe supports us as the soil supports the expression of the seeds that are planted in it. As I pass these seeds to you, take one and contemplate what wants to be done through you this year. Consider not only the activity itself but the quality of being that you want to express through your work. When you are clear about what wants to be accomplished through you, write it on the green paper and fold it into the size of a tiny seed. Holding the paper seed and the real seed, repeat after me: 'I accept the blessing of life on that which I commit to bring forth through me. May the creative energy of the universe flow through me as I dedicate my time, my energy, and my love to the work to be done through my hands and heart.'

"Now remove your candle from the pot; plant both seeds, the paper and the actual one, in the soil; write your name on the pot, and replace the candle as a symbol of the light that will be multiplied through your work."

When participants finish, the leader or a helper collects the pots and places them back on the altar.

Leader: "Please hold the symbols of your work in your lap and perform the self blessing along with me."

The following blessing should be duplicated before the ritual so each participant has a copy to take home.

Leader: "Become still. Close your eyes.

"Holding your hands and arms out, palms up, repeat after me:'I receive the light of Spirit in my mind, my body, and in all that I do. I open myself to be renewed so that I may give forth the gifts that are mine to give.'

"Holding your hands over your eyes, repeat after me: 'I bless my eyes that they may see the radiance of God everywhere I look. The veil is pulled from my sight, and I behold everyone and everything as sacred.'

"Holding your hands on your forehead, repeat after me: 'My mind is the mind of God. I think creative, visionary, life-enhancing thoughts that are for the good of all and for the accomplishment of my work. I accept the call to do the work that is mine to do, and to work for the transformation of consciousness on earth.'

"Holding your hands on the tools of your work, repeat after me:'I bless these tools of my work. I purify and sanctify them to do holy, empowering, peaceful work through me. Once again I commit myself to accomplish what is mine to do with the help of God.'

"Holding your hands on your lips, repeat after me: 'I speak with the power, the truth, and the wisdom of God. Only words that heal, strengthen, create benefit, and connect pass through my lips. The word of God is spoken through me.'

"Holding your hands over your heart, repeat after me: 'My heart is overflowing with compassion for the world and all the beings of the earth. My love is everlasting. It can hold anything; it heals everything.'

"Holding your hands, palms together in front of your heart in the traditional gesture of prayer, repeat after me: 'I am the light of the world. I freely give my light to everyone. I am drawn to divine service in perfect ways for myself and for those I serve. My will is to do the work that is mine to do. I am renewed, lifted up, filled with the light of God. This light now pours from my eyes, my hands, and my heart in a shining river. Blessed is all that I have been given and all that I now have to give. So it is now and forever more. Blessed be.'"

Leader lights the candles in the pots on the altar as the self blessing is concluded and participants still have their eyes closed.

Leader: "See the garden of light that has sprung up because of your dedication and commitment. May all that you have spoken come into your life for the good of all and the harm of none. As we conclude, remember to take your pot with its seeds. Water it and know that all that has been planted grows perfectly. Also take with you a copy of the self blessing to remind yourself of what you accept from the life all around you. May you and your work be blessed this year."

Spring Equinox Celebration

The spring equinox celebrates new life from seeming death. This celebration of Persephone rising, of seeds sprouting, of resurrection, moves us from the cold, dense, earthbound energy of winter to the airy dawn of spring. This ritual works well for a family, group, or spiritual community, with children as well as adults. However, if you are celebrating the spring equinox by yourself, you can do all the creation, planting, praying, and contemplating with only you and the energy of new beginnings that spring represents. In the part of the ritual that honors children, you can honor the child that you once were.

Materials:

Sprouted fava beans in a pot
Bouquets of spring flowers
Bobby pins and florist ties
Edible flowers from health food stores or markets
Prayer flags attached to poles
Colored eggs

Set up:

Prepare a table for the ceremonial breakfast.

Place a pot of sprouted fava beans at each person's setting.

Prepare a breakfast or brunch feast with plenty of egg dishes.

Wash the edible flowers and place in a bowl.

Place some of the spring flowers in vases and scatter others around the feast table.

Hide colored eggs if children will be present.

About a week to ten days before the spring equinox ritual, ask the participants to prepare prayers of new beginnings for themselves and the world. Whether they do this individually or in a group, each person should search his heart and determine what wants to come forth through him as new beginnings, new projects, or new ways of being. Each person then writes these desires in words or symbols on sproutable fava beans and plants the beans in the moist soil of a pot. *(Fava beans can be found in health food stores or garden supply stores, or they can be saved and dried from the previous fall. Do not use blanched or packaged beans as they will not sprout.)* The participants write their name on their pot and may decorate it any way they wish. Make sure the soil and seeds are kept moist during the days leading to the ritual.

The day before the ritual, ask the participants to meditate on the miracle of creation, how the life that germinates the beans also creates the results of their desires. They should also discern their deepest wishes for the earth and all its living creatures.

Each person should create a prayer flag for the ritual by decorating a gauzy piece of material, about fifteen inches square, with their prayers in words, symbols, or pictures drawn on the material. They can attach this flag to a dowel, a small pole, or even a chopstick.

The night before the celebration, the participants may choose to color eggs. Natural dye from beets, berries, or the brown papery outside layer of onions will give the eggs an old-fashioned appearance, though store-bought Easter egg dye can also be used.

Decorating eggs can be a time for participants to discuss how it must have been for ancient people who, having just gone through the cold, dark winter, wandered the thawed land in search of fresh eggs.

Before dawn on the morning of the equinox, the participants bring their flags and pots with the sprouted beans to the home or meeting place where the breakfast celebration is to take place. They may also bring spring flower displays, edible flowers, and colored eggs. Taking their prayer flags outside to a hillside, a field, or even to a backyard, they wait for the dawn together.

Leader: "The dawn of the day that brings more light than darkness is about to break. We have looked forward to spring, and it is almost here. Let us take a moment to remember the dark wintertime that is about to end. As ancient people did for thousands of years, we, too, rested, reflected, and told stories indoors as we moved through the winter with the love of our family and community. Unlike our ancestors, though, we did not have to worry that our food would run out or that our fire would extinguish. Whatever our winter struggle was this year, it was not like the struggle of our ancestors, and so we honor them at this time.

"We are about to rise up with the dawn, as Persephone rose from the realm of the dead. Before the sun rises and the morning of our rebirth begins, let us retell the story of Persephone, because her story is our story. *(Note: another resurrection story, such as that of Inanna or Jesus, may be substituted.)*

"It was in autumn that the black chariot of Hades broke through the earth from the underworld. His black stallions leapt from the realm below to the field of flowers where Persephone and her mother, Demeter, were passing the beautiful day. Hades snatched the lovely Persephone and took her to his realm of the dead to be his queen.

"Through the millennia, Persephone has grown into a powerful queen who journeys with the heroes of antiquity and also with us when we plumb the depths of our own subconscious to gain the power that comes from self-knowledge. But today is her time to return to her mother and to us on the surface of this beautiful planet, to the new life that comes with spring.

"The life in us is ready to leap into new endeavors with the increased energy that comes with the perennial rebirth of life. We imagine Persephone coming to the surface, not dropped off from the chariot that carried her away, but shot up through a crevice in the earth like a gushing spring or an erupting volcano. She arrives on the land with a leap into her mother's arms and into the lushness of spring.

" And so when the rays of the sun break over the horizon, let us leap up and shout for joy: 'Spring is come!'"

When the sun's rays appear, everyone leaps, jumps, dances, sings, and shouts joyously. If the group must wait a few extra minutes for the sun to appear, a song can be sung in the interim, or people can share what quality their leaping will have, such as "I will leap for my freedom," or "I will jump up with great love," or "I will spring into my new work."

When the leaping and cavorting subside, the leader continues.

Leader: "This beautiful morning carries with it the collective consciousness of our ancestors for tens of thousands of years. They believed that new beginnings were supported by the energy of the beginning of spring. You have with you the prayers for the world written and drawn on your prayer flags. Lift them up now, and let the rays of the new sun of spring beam through your prayers, shining their power over the world. Please share with all of us your wishes for the earth and her people."

Everyone shares their prayers for the world as they lift their prayer flags to the sun. After everyone has spoken, the leader continues.

Leader: "May it be that these prayers are carried on the breezes of spring around the world. May they find their manifestation in perfect ways and in perfect places that cry out for these wishes. May we all hold that a new beginning for the world is possible this spring."

Everyone then takes their prayer flags back to the home or meeting place where breakfast is to be served. If children are a part of this ceremony, they hunt for the eggs that have been hidden. The prayer flags are planted in the yard or placed in a tall vase as a centerpiece for the table. Everyone helps prepare the meal, which should include several egg dishes and a salad made from baby greens and the edible flowers. This salad should be served in a clear glass bowl so that the purples, oranges, yellows, and reds of the flowers can be seen and appreciated.

When the meal is ready, everyone sits down with their pot of sprouts on the plate in front of them.

Leader: "We celebrate the mystery of new life from seeming death on this holiday. Our ancestors buried their dead in the earth, just as they planted their seeds, knowing that new life springs forth from fertile soil. This reminded them, as it reminds us, that our loved ones who have passed on are immortal and have not died to remain dead, but have transformed into their resurrected selves, living and expressing themselves in realms beyond this earthly life. Just as they did when their time came, we, too, will go through the doorway called death to be resurrected into our new life, our new spring.

"To celebrate new life today we will eat the living shoots of the beans we have planted and the living flowers in our salad. In front of you is the pot with your germinated beans. You wrote an intention or a desire on the beans as you planted them. The power of life has created green sprouts from the beans just as it is busy creating the results of your desire. In order to magnify the power of this creative endeavor, I invite you to eat a sprout or two and put the rest in the salad for us all.

"As we pass the salad bowl around, please speak an intention you have sprouted for yourself and what that generalized wish might be for us all. Before we pass the bowl, however, so you may be with the magic of your own creation, please take a few moments to remember what you wrote on the beans as you planted them and put your hands around their pot. Recall the desire in you for a new expression or experience. Know that this desire was planted in you by the same force that caused the bean to grow and that will ultimately create your wish for you. Carefully break off one of the sprouts now and ingest it along with its surging life force and power of creation, knowing that the living energy in the sprout combines with your life force and magnifies the power of the manifestation of your desire."

Everyone does this.

Leader. "We now pass the salad bowl around; please break off another sprout or two and share your wishes as you add your sprout to the salad."

After it is done, the pots of beans are removed from the table. The salad of flowers, greens, and sprouts is lightly dressed and served with the rest of the meal. During the meal the leader speaks again.

Leader: "This holiday, which ancient people called Ostara, is named after a goddess of spring. Ostara's symbols were eggs, chicks, and bunnies, symbols of fertility and new life. As a holiday celebrating new life, Ostara is a celebration of babies and children, so let us honor our children. I invite all parents to share the wonderful qualities of their children so that we may all appreciate and love them with you."

The parents speak about the unique and special qualities of their children, as the meal continues.

When the meal is complete everyone makes flower garlands or hair decorations out of the fresh flowers that are strewn on the table and in the vases. Men, women, and children all decorate each other with the beauty of spring. When the festivities are complete, all leave with their symbols of spring and earthly blessing.

. *Ritual for Lovers* .

This ritual is for two people who love each other. The perfect celebration of passion, it is appropriate for Valentine's Day, an anniversary, reconnecting after an argument, or evolving a relationship into sexual expression.

Materials:

Candles

A bowl of rose petals

A variety of scented essential oils and lotions

Pure water

Honey or maple syrup

An image of a deity, if desired

Set up:

Wear loose, comfortable clothes, or wear nothing at all.

Set the temperature in the room for comfort.

Create an altar with the materials listed above.

*T*o begin, the lovers create a circle of rose petals on the floor or on a bed, large enough for both to be seated within. Although you may follow this ritual verbatim, it is simple enough to paraphrase the theme of each blessing and use your own words.

✢

Participants (to each other): "We create this circle of love to sanctify our bodies and the sacred pleasure we will share. We ask all the deities of love to be with us as we share the gift of sensual and spiritual delight."

Light the candles and speak of the fire in your hearts.

Participants: "May this candle be the symbol of the firestorm of passion I have within me for you, my beloved."

Sitting across from each other, gaze into each others' eyes and bow, speaking of the divinity you perceive in your beloved.

Participants: "I see the face of God when I look in your face. In your eyes I see lifetimes of love. Thank you for being in my life now."

Taking a drop of essential oil, anoint each others' hearts. Speak of what you wish for your beloved's heart and what you know is in your own heart.

Participants: "May the love I feel for you open your heart so that the whole universe may pass through it and be blessed. My own heart holds so much love for you that the love overflows and blesses the world and everyone in it with every breath I take."

After each blessing, gaze into each others' eyes and breathe together for a few breaths.

Taking a good amount of lotion, massage each others' hands and bless them, speaking your wish for the beloved's hands and your own.

Participants: "May your hands be blessed by everything they touch. May our touching be so complete that there is no boundary between us. May my hands bring you only pleasure so that you are transported into realms beyond this world."

Breathe together, and fall into each others' eyes.

Taking the honey or maple syrup, touch each others' mouths and bless the words and kisses that come from those lips.

Participants: "May only sweetness pour from your mouth. May our kisses together arouse the passion of Venus herself. May my words always empower and honor you, my love."

Breathe and gaze at each other for a long moment.

Taking some drops of water, dab the water on each others' eyes, saying your wishes for their seeing.

Participants: "This pure water washes any shadow from your sight; you see me as I am with all my good qualities and those qualities yet to be expressed. I see in you the highest and greatest aspects of your soul and all the ways you struggle. May our sight be washed in love so all that we see in each other is precious."

Pause, breathe and gaze.

Taking the oil once more, anoint each others' foreheads in the place of the third eye.

Participants: "May our lovemaking open worlds of perception for you. May you know the way things are in the realm of the absolute because of the pleasure that moves through our bodies and souls. May we be changed at the depth of our being, and may the world be blessed."

Gaze into each others' eyes, bow to each other, and make sweet love together.

. *Midsummer Celebration* .

Midsummer celebrates the fullness of lush, growing energy. The day when the hours of light are the longest and the darkness is the shortest, it is associated with the sun, fairies, trickery, and deep love. This celebration covers a full twenty-four hour period, but you may select elements of the complete celebration for a shorter ritual. This is a perfect celebration for a group of families who play or vacation together regularly. It would also be appropriate for a spiritual community or summer camp participants who may not know each other well. If you are a single person who celebrates the summer solstice, simply use the leader's words as your directions and do the blessings for those around the world in your heart. Spend the day outdoors in the sun; bring enough food for breakfast, lunch, and dinner, and don't forget the sun block.

Materials:

    Overnight provisions for all participants
    Food for breakfast, lunch, dinner, and snacks
    Wood for a bonfire, or any substitute for a bonfire
    Outdoor games or sports equipment
    Yellow and golden flowers, florist ties, shiny streamers
    Surprise gifts
    Globe of the earth

A chart of the time zones around the world
Sun block and plenty of drinking water
Patio umbrellas

*P*articipants of the Midsummer Celebration congregate on Midsummer's Eve, the evening before the summer solstice, at the home or retreat facility where the celebration is to take place. The facilitator for the evening begins by leading a discussion about fairies.

☖

Leader: "Ancient people knew that the fairy kingdom drew especially near to the human kingdom at the time of Midsummer. We all have read fairy tales and folk tales about fairies. Usually the fairies from these tales are small human-like beings with wings; they seem fragile and beautiful. However, people of ancient cultures who felt a close connection with fairies thought them to be wild beings, usually associated with natural realms of forests, water, and earth. Some people believe that fairies were here long before humans came to the earth, and though helpful to humans, they are also mischievous, sometimes troublesome, sometimes quite frightening; they do not abide by appropriate human behavior."

Depending on the age and familiarity of the participants with various literary depictions of fairies, the group could talk about Tinkerbell, Puck, or other fairies they have heard or read about, drawing their own conclusions about fairies. As bedtime approaches, anyone who wants to leave a snack for the fairies can prepare it and leave it out where the fairies are sure to find it. In the morning, the snacks should be gone and replaced by funny gifts from the fairies.

Awakening before sunrise, the group goes to a natural outdoor space where a bonfire can be built and kept burning all day and evening. Alternatively, a fire could be built in a barbecue or another metal container outside on a patio. If no open fires are possible, a collection of votive candles can be used. A breakfast picnic is also prepared and brought to the fire site.

Leader: "Ancient people lit huge fires on this day to honor the life-giving properties of the sun, that sustains all life on earth. The warmth and brightness of our fire mirrors the warmth and brilliance of the sun. As I light our fire now, I light it in honor of all fires lit on this day throughout all the summers of human life on earth. I light it in honor of the day with the most light. May this light also shine in us."

The fire is lit.

Leader: "Let us also honor the sun as it rises on this longest day. Today we are here for its first rays, and we will be here for its last. We will live in the sun this entire day, feeling its warmth and appreciating its nurturing qualities. As the sun rises, let us face it so that the brilliance of its light may break directly on us."

Everyone faces the sun with their hands raised. When the first rays shoot over the horizon. the leader continues.

Leader: "Welcome, Sun. Welcome, all the deities who are representations of the sun. Welcome, Shamash of Mesopotamia. Welcome, Ra of Egypt. Welcome, Vishnu of India. Welcome, Apollo of Greece. Welcome, Mithras of Persia. Welcome, Sol Invictus of Rome. Welcome, Christ of Galilee. And welcome, Prometheus, a mortal who stole fire from the gods and brought it to us. We celebrate you, Sun, on this your longest day. May we always give thanks for your illumination, your life-giving energy, your endless generosity. May we see ourselves as brothers and sisters of all who receive your healing rays today. Blessed be."

The food for breakfast is blessed and eating begins. During breakfast, a conversation ensues about how the sun participated in creating the food that is consumed. Also, the gifts from the fairies can be shared.

After breakfast the leader brings out the globe and demonstrates the earth's path around the sun, using the bonfire to represent the sun. The leader also demonstrates how the revolving of our earth creates night and day and how the seasons are created by the tilt of the planet as it follows its orbit.

Leader: "This longest day of the year is experienced by everyone in the northern hemisphere, for whom much of the day has already passed. In fact, in some places it is already tomorrow morning. We are going to bless all of our brothers and sisters on our planet as we all experience the solstice here today, with a special blessing to those in the southern hemisphere who today experience their shortest day in the middle of their winter. We will now bless those in places that have already passed noon. For those places that have not reached noon, we will bless those people as their noon arrives."

The leader then discusses the countries in the first time zone, explaining what time it is at the moment. (A complete list of the world's time zones can be found online at www.world-timezone.com.) For example, on the west coast of the United States, this part of the ritual would probably be taking place around 6:00 a.m. Therefore, in the first time zone, which includes New Zealand and western China, it would be 2:00 a.m. the following morning. The participants discuss what is probably going on for those people in the first time zone. If anyone has friends or family in that zone, they may share that information. Blessings are said for those people, and then the next time zone is considered. The participants should have a clear sense of the people living, working, sleeping, and tending their families the world over as each country and its inhabitants are blessed. If there is conflict occurring in a particular country, special prayers are offered. By the time the group circles most of the world, perhaps to the Greenland time zone or western Canada, it would be noon there.

After this blessing the group takes a break and has some free time. However, as the hour turns and it becomes noon in the next western time zone, the group reconvenes for the blessing for those countries. As the noon hour comes into the United States, more family and friends will be identified for special blessings.

By the time it is noon, lunch is prepared and served. It is appropriate for this lunch to consist of food echoing the heat of the sun, such as oranges or melons cut in circles, and spicy food such as Mexican or Indian fare. Have sunblock available, and set up patio or beach umbrellas for people who do not want to spend the entire day in the sun.

During the afternoon, the blessing of the people in the remaining time zones is accomplished. This afternoon time is for active outdoor games and lazy napping. The gold flowers, shiny streamers, and florist ties are brought out for everyone to make crowns symbolic of the yellow, beaming sun for themselves or others. The shiny streamers will reflect the rays of the sun until the group resembles streaming sunbeams.

At dinnertime, the fire that has been replenished all day becomes the grill for the meal of roasted foods. After dinner marshmallows may be brought out for roasting.

The leader begins the closing part of the solstice ritual.

Leader: "The time of sundown is almost here; the longest day of the year is almost at an end. As brilliant and filled with light as this day has been, the setting sun reminds us that nothing on this earth lasts forever. Everything is in the flow of change as the seasons of the year turn and as the seasons of our lives turn. Most of us love the light, the warmth, the vigor of the growing season, but just as the season of our youth passes, so does the light give way to darkness as the passing solstice moves us closer to the seasons of autumn and winter. With the sunset this evening the darkness will grow for half a year until the germ of the light is born again in the depth of winter. Although that time seems a long way off, its preparation starts now.

"This is a good time to acknowledge those things in our life that we love that will not stay as they are. It is a good time to appreciate the transitory blessings of life. Each one of us will have an opportunity to speak of something that we love that will pass. As we do this, we increase our ability to love in the present and let go into the next moment freely and with appreciation. Now I invite you to share your blessings so that we may feel them in our own hearts. As each person shares, I offer you the globe to hold as you speak."

The globe is passed to the first person and on around until everyone has had a chance to share. The members of the group share such things as, "I love my children. Sometimes I wish they would stay little, but each stage that they grow into is even more precious to me," or "I wish that no more species would become extinct on our planet," or "I will miss my old dog when she passes." As the sky darkens the group is led more and more deeply into their hearts. When everyone has shared their thoughts and feelings the leader concludes.

Leader: "This completes our solstice celebration. We have celebrated the sun, the heat, the light, our brothers and sisters around the globe; we have eaten, played, and rested together; we have shared the precious, flowing, and changing blessings of our lives. We are filled and content. Blessed be."

. *First Harvest Celebration* .

For as long as grain has been domesticated, the blessing of the first grain cut and the bread made from it have constituted holy acts. The blessing and eating of the bread in this ritual is reminiscent of the Christian communion, but this ceremony actually has its roots in a much earlier time. Ideally set outside, this ritual could be performed indoors without the cornmeal. It may also be performed in a shortened version with just the honoring and eating of the bread, as the blessing before a late summer meal. If you are celebrating by yourself, you could make a personal ritual out of stirring, kneading, and baking bread, eating the first bite as you read the meditation in this ceremony. Instead of speaking the personal stories aloud, you could write them in a journal.

Materials:

    A loaf of dense bread that can be torn without crumbling

    At least two pounds of cornmeal

    Other symbols of the season as desired

Set up:

    Create an outdoor altar containing the bread, cornmeal, and other objects of grain, such as ears of corn, stalks of wheat and corn dollies.

*T*he participants gather in a circle around the altar. The leader creates a space by sprinkling the cornmeal in a circle around the group and altar. The leader should be sure to be in the circle without needing to step over the line to get back in.

✦

Leader: "We create a sacred circle for our work today honoring the cycle of the grain, which includes its planting, growing, harvesting, and consumption. We give thanks to the grain that so willingly gives its body to be sacrificed so that the people who tended it when it was growing and others can be fed. As I create this circle with bits of harvested corn, know with me that our ritual today is centered in holy time and holy space. We consciously take leave of our normal days and enter the realm of the holy ones who represented the grain harvest to our ancestors. We call upon the god Lugh to be with us, as well as Demeter, Ceres, Corn Woman and John Barleycorn."

After the circle has been created, the leader goes to the center and takes the bread from the altar.

Leader: "This bread symbolizes the unconditional support we have on earth. We bless and give thanks for this bread now. Its form nourishes our form and reminds us that anything we need is already given. Surely the formless as well is all around us now—ideas, guidance, support, connection, and the qualities of beauty, love, joy, peace, creativity, and harmony. As I break the bread, we are reminded that, in addition to all the blessings of life that we enjoy, there are also sorrows. Each of us has been broken by the unhappiness and grief that comes with life. It is part of the mystery that, in our brokenness, the blessings of love and connection often have a chance to go more deeply into us. We are broken open to be filled with love."

Leader breaks the bread.

Leader: "As I give each of you a piece of this bread, hold it in your hands and reflect on where it has been."

Chunks of bread that are big enough for several bites are passed out.

Leader: "This bread was made from dough which, in turn, was made from ground wheat. The wheat was originally in the form of individual kernels growing on a stalk with many other kernels and many stalks growing out of the center of one plant. This wheat plant was born in the spring as a single sprout poking up to the light. The sprout pushed its way out of a single kernel planted in the earth. I ask you now to lie on your backs on the earth, with your heads in the center of the circle and your piece of bread on your chest."

Everyone repositions themselves on the ground with their heads pointing to the center of the circle and their feet well within the circle of cornmeal.

Leader: "Imagine you are a kernel of wheat planted a few inches beneath the surface of the earth. It is dark and moist in the earth, and you have a rumbling within you to move and grow. Instinctually, you split the side of your kernel's sheath and send a tiny white root down deep into the dark, moist earth. Feel the tendrils of little white roots move from your body into the earth beneath you, seeking nourishment. Then, with the intelligence moving within you, send a small green shoot up, seeking the light that you know is there. Feel the green shoot move up to the light and break the surface of the earth. Feel the sunlight stream down onto your little green body, calling it up, up, as your roots go down, down. Over the days and nights, you grow into a sturdy plant with hundreds of kernels of wheat waving on your stalks. You have made yourself out of a single kernel with the assistance of the earth's nutrients, sunlight, water, and your inherent nature. Experience how it feels to be a wheat plant for a few moments."

Pause.

Leader: "Raise yourself now; come back to yourself, and eat a bite of your bread realizing that the bread becomes your body as it is digested. Realize, too, that your body is made of earth, water, sunlight, and spiritual intelligence. Feel the earth in your body; feel the rivers in your body; feel the sunlight in each cell; know that the power of life directs every living process."

Everyone takes a bite of their bread.

Leader: "This bread represents the entire harvest, billions and billions of kernels of wheat, an unlimited abundance. The bread nourishes your body so that you can have harvests in your own life. Move now into groups of three or four and prepare to share with your group what you are harvesting in your life this season. As you share your stories with your group, offer each person a bite of your bread. Thus we eat of each others' lives and are nourished by each other."

Participants combine into groups, offering each other their bread and telling what they have created in their lives.

Leader: "This bread also is a symbol of all earthly blessings that we use, enjoy, and share. What are you grateful for in this moment? What is a divine gift that you love or what is a hurt that you have healed through? Share your blessings with your group as you give them another bite of your bread. We share our delights and our healings with each other, and they are multiplied."

Everyone follows this instruction. The leader replenishes anyone's bread if he or she runs out.

Leader: "Just as the wheat has given its life for you, you are giving your life for all that you are harvesting. Your time and energy are given away each day for your activities. Contemplate now: is your harvest a pleasing way to have given your life? As you eat the last of your bread, make a vow that the life nourished by this bite of bread will be spent in the highest of ways. What will that way be? What healing will be facilitated by this bread? What high purpose will be expressed? What gift to humanity will this bread serve? What will you do with this small but essential unit of your precious life energy?"

Each person tells the whole group what they will do with this bit of life energy that will serve and bless themselves and others. After this the leader concludes.

Leader: "We have honored the life cycle on earth; we have declared what we have created in our lives; we have given thanks for our blessings and our healings; we have committed to give our life for a high purpose. May it be that the power of life that knows how to create hundreds of kernels from one, takes our intentions and multiplies them a hundredfold so that great, great good comes from our lives. With our work blessed and complete let us now break the circle and resume our familiar lives."

Everyone scatters the cornmeal as a completion of the ritual.

. *Fall Equinox Celebration* .

The Fall Equinox Celebration at the end of the harvest expresses gratitude toward the earth for so generously giving us our food. Another important theme is restoring balance on our planet, since this is one of the two times of the year when light and dark are exactly balanced. This ritual is written for a family, a group of families, a community organization, or a spiritual group. If you are celebrating alone, read the leader's words to guide your own contemplation.

Materials:

    A blanket

    A wrapped gift from each person

    A special family dish from each person

    Dry leaves

    Markers

    A ceremonial bowl

Set up:

    Spread the blanket out on the floor.

    Set the table for the harvest feast.

    The dry leaves should be strewn about the table along with traditional harvest vegetables such as squash and corn.

*D*uring the day leading up to the harvest meal, the participants should perform an act of restoration together in honor of their effort to restore balance to the world. Some suggestions include cleaning trash from a trail or neighborhood, helping an elderly person with home maintenance, serving a meal at a soup kitchen, writing letters for a worthy cause, or planting a tree. Any caring act done with the intent of restoring balance to the world qualifies. For other ideas, contact a local volunteer agency. If the group is large, more than one project might be accomplished.

When the celebrants arrive at the home or meeting place for the harvest meal, they each place a gift on the blanket. These will be used in a ceremony reminiscent of a Native American custom called a "Give Away," in which everyone brings something special to them that they are prepared to give away.

After the meal is prepared, it is blessed by the leader.

Leader: "Tonight we gratefully celebrate the harvest of the earth. We honor the seeds from last year's harvest that has become the fruits, vegetables, and grains of this year; we honor the sowing and nurturing of the food that we eat tonight; we honor the lives of the animals that are a part of our meal; we honor the cooks. We give thanks for all the loving care that has gone before this moment allowing us to celebrate tonight with this food and good company. We honor the friendship and love in this room; we honor our bodies that will use this food to maintain health and strength so that we all may accomplish what we are on earth to do. Let us enjoy this meal, and, as we do, I ask each person to speak about the dish they have contributed. Tell us about your family who originally prepared it and how you feel when you eat it. Let this harvest meal be one of gratitude for our family homes."

Everyone begins the meal while telling the stories of their family and the dish they are sharing. As the meal continues, the leader speaks.

Leader: "At this equinox celebration we honor the balance of light and dark. We use this powerful time of the year to enhance balance in the world. We know that we deplete resources; we take advantage of others, sometimes unknowingly; often we use more than our share. Our philanthropic efforts this afternoon were offered to balance our use of this wonderful planet. Let us talk of what we gave back today."

As they complete the meal, each person speaks about the work that they accomplished to balance the world and how it made them feel. In between dinner and dessert the leader facilitates this releasing process.

Leader: "The autumn season is often called 'fall.' As leaves fall from the trees, we let fall away from us that which we no longer need."

Each person takes a dry leaf and a marker. (The markers should be moist and soft enough so as not to crumble the leaves.)

Leader: "Now, close your eyes, and let that which needs to fall away be revealed to you. It could be a project, a relationship, a way of being. Let the release be as effortless as a leaf falling from the tree. When you are ready, write on your leaf a word or symbol for that which you are releasing."

Pause until everyone has done this.

Leader: "As I pass this bowl, I invite you to crumble your leaf into the bowl, and, if you like, tell us what you are letting fall away."

Everyone does this.

Dessert is served. At the end of the evening the leader concludes the ritual.

Leader: "As we have experienced, the autumn equinox is a time of letting go. It is also a time of receiving, as we have done in celebrating the harvest. The closing part of this celebration is about letting go in generosity and receiving in gratitude, a wonderful act of balance.

"The 'Give Away' is a ritual of passing on something that has had much meaning for us with the hope that it will mean a great deal to the person who receives it. These gifts on the blanket are just objects, but they carry with them great significance. What you receive is no accident; it is especially for you. Everyone come forward and take your gift."

Everyone takes a gift at the same time and opens it. Stories are shared about the meaning of the gifts and the appropriateness of the gift for its new owner.

Everyone helps clean up the meal so that balance is restored in the kitchen.

. *Family Ritual at Halloween* .

This celebration, encompassing the evening of Halloween, honors our dear ones who have died. Though this ritual is written here for family and friends of the departed, it is also a perfect ritual to perform by yourself, alone. Sometimes the connection with a loved one who has passed on is easier when the distraction of other people is not present. If you do this ritual alone, wait until the trick-or-treaters have all gone home. Then spend some time relaxing into a meditative state before reading the words of the ritual leader. Read through one complete section of the ritual until you have the sense of it in your mind, and then allow your inner self to take over. Continue with each section of the ritual in this way, or let your communion with your loved one guide you.

Materials:

    A meal of foods that the deceased person or people enjoyed
    Objects reminiscent of these beloved ones
    Photos of the family members to be honored
    A large pot or cauldron
    Paper and writing instruments for each person
    A bowl of water or a crystal ball
    Halloween candy for trick-or-treaters

A fire in a fireplace or a cluster of candles

Set up:
Build an altar including the bowl of water or crystal ball.
Have candy ready for trick-or-treaters.
Place the cauldron and pens by the fireplace or candles.

*A*s the guests or family members arrive, have them place on the altar photos of their departed loved ones and the objects that were precious to them. Depending on how many people will be participating, you can plan the meal as a potluck, asking participants to bring a dish that was loved by their dearly departed. As the meal is blessed, the host or leader explains a bit about the ancient holiday. This job could also be given to a child.

☿

Leader: "This night of all nights was the most holy to ancient people. It marked the end of a cycle and was the night when the veil between the worlds was the thinnest. Ancient people believed that on this night they could contact their dear ones who had preceded them into the spirit realm. They believed that their own intuition was the keenest on this night, aided, perhaps, by the voices of those who had died.

"Our symbols of Halloween are actually ancient and had very different meanings in the old times. Jack-o-lanterns were the lanterns used to show spirits who walked on the land this night the way back home. Treats were offerings left for the spirits of the relatives, and tricks were punishments meted out to those who forgot to leave a treat for their departed family member. Costumes were worn if you wanted to disguise yourself from your relatives. The witch of Halloween is what has become of the wise crone, the aged bearer of the wisdom of the culture. Her cauldron was the magic pot that took all the dead things and transformed them into new life. It was a night of great holiness, intuition, guidance, and love for departed family.

"We keep the old traditions alive tonight. We begin by blessing this meal and honoring the beloved ones we remember as we eat the food that they loved."

During the meal, tell stories about the family members you are honoring. Tell about the foods you are eating and the memories they evoke. Participants should feel as if the deceased are actually present at the table.

As the meal is being eaten, it may be interrupted by trick-or-treaters. Offer these young strangers treats in the spirit of your celebration, remembering the relatives you are honoring and the fleeting nature of earthly life. Rather than accommodate the grabbing of candy so that the trick-or-

treaters can hurry to the next house, encourage eye contact with the trick-or-treater while offering the treat, and say something like "May your life on earth be as sweet as this candy."

After the meal, everyone should retrieve their objects and photos from the altar and take a paper and pen. Everyone gather by the fireplace or light candles on a table. Let the only light in the room be from the flames. Going around the group, each person tells why the object they chose is a precious reminder of his or her loved one. Tell about when the photo was taken and pass it around. Share the qualities that were most characteristic of your loved one and gaze at the photo, remembering everything you can about your relative and letting ideas associate that may or may not be actual memories. The leader invites everyone into the following meditation, speaking very slowly with pauses after each suggestion.

Leader: "Please get very comfortable and let your eyes gently close. Become aware of your breathing and follow your breath as it flows effortlessly in and out of your body. Let your entire body relax and become warm and heavy. Imagine that you are growing roots from your body into the earth, little tendrils that grow down, down to the energy of Mother Earth. That energy flows up and into your body through the roots so your body becomes grounded as your mind and heart become free. Imagine that you rise and float to the edges of this room where you will sprinkle salt crystals in the corners. Know that this room is a completely safe place, and only the ideas and energies that we invite may enter. As you sprinkle the salt, the room changes to one from your past, a room where you were once with your loved one. See every detail about this room; smell the air in this room; feel the temperature and quality of the space. Sit in a favorite place of yours, and call to the spirit of your relative in your heart. Ask your relative to come and be with you. As you feel the presence of your loved one come around you, tell him or her you have some things to share and some things to ask. In a moment I will be silent for several minutes, all the time you need for a complete experience. You may use this time to ask your loved one anything; you may tell him about you and your life now; you may go on a journey with your loved one; you may ask his advice about your life. I will call you back after a few minutes."

Let there be silence for five to ten minutes if children are present, longer if the group is more experienced in meditation.

Leader: "You may ask your loved one if there is anything else that is important to know at this time. *(Pause)* Express your gratitude, your love, and your thanks to your loved one, and wish him well. *(Pause)* I am going to clap my hands three times and when I do the room will change back to this room on this day."

Leader claps gently three times. If desired, people can share their experiences. Occasionally someone will get a message for someone else in the room.

Leader: "We will now celebrate the ending of the ancient year by releasing anything we do not wish to bring forward with us into this precious, fallow time of winter darkness and then into the new year of creation. Please consider what projects are complete, what relationships are complete, what wants to end in your life, which ways of being you are ready to release, and what has had sufficient energy and time spent on it. What can you release so that its energy may be freed up for new endeavors in the future? Please write what you are releasing on the paper."

All pause and do this.

Leader: "Place your papers in the cauldron. The black cauldron is the magical pot of the Celtic goddess Cerridwen who takes everything that has died and stirs it in her bubbling pot. From this mixture comes new life in different form."

The leader symbolically stirs the pot and then burns the papers in the fireplace or sets them on fire from a candle.

Leader: "As the old is destroyed, it is transformed into pure creative potential for our next endeavors. Life, death, and life again is the law. Let us pause and feel the lightness of release. That which no longer served us is gone, and we are free."

Pause.

Leader: "Our final ritual tonight is the ancient practice of *scrying*. Before scientific inquiry became prominent, ancient people opened to their inner wisdom by peering into a bowl of water or a crystal. What they saw gave them important information for themselves or others. Tonight we honor this ancient practice as a way to open to our deep knowing, our intuition. Tonight we have already traveled to places far beyond our normal waking consciousness, and so our inner eyes are opened. We gaze into the *scrying* object with no agenda whatsoever, that whatever is revealed to us may be interesting and valuable."

With the scrying *object visible to everyone and the room lit only by candlelight or firelight, the Leader continues.*

Leader: "Again, become completely relaxed and follow your next few breaths in and out. Feel the little roots that anchor your body to the earth, and allow your eyes to become half-closed and very soft. Look easily into the water/crystal and let your mind wander. Images may come to you; words may be heard; an intuitive feeling may come upon you. Remember, you are safe and protected by your ancestors."

Let the gazing continue for several minutes before the Leader concludes.

Leader: "Please close your eyes now and let any images fade away. Recall the room around you. When I clap three times, you will be once again in your normal waking consciousness."

The leader gently claps three times. Anyone who wants may share his or her experience.

Leader: "We honor the ancestors, our relatives and friends who have gone before us into the next experience. May we be guided by their love as we live here on earth. May we nurture our intuition and intelligence and not be deceived by circumstances, for we are all guided and protected by the power of life. When our time comes, may we go through the door of death with the peace that is in our hearts right now. Blessed be."

Everyone should have dessert, a cup of something warm, or even just a drink of water. Turn the lights on. Pack up the objects that were brought. Everyone might help clean up the kitchen so that waking consciousness fully returns and people are feeling quite comfortable before they leave.

Part Three

The Transitions of Life

. *Wheel of Passages* .

You may think of "rites of passage" as ceremonies other cultures perform to initiate young people into adulthood. Unfortunately, the Western world has all but lost the idea that the trials and passages of life can and should be prepared for and celebrated; it is possible, if not advantageous, to undergo them and then come out the other side changed.

You experience many rites of passage in your lifetime. These include getting your driver's license, graduating from school, getting married, getting divorced, having a career and retiring. You will ultimately die, which is also a rite of passage. Yet these journeys may fail to nurture your soul because you have not deepened them with the respect they deserve, thus losing the opportunity to deepen yourself in the process.

Rites-of-passage rituals simulate the hero's journey, a flow of events that include a hero, a villian, a task or challenge, and a victory. The hero's journey is found in myth, fable, and real life. Ritualizing this moment through challenge allows the changes in you to take root at a deeper level. Without such rituals, the passages of your life remain unacknowledged milestones. Life may become so impoverished that you subconsciously seek the hero's journey in inappropriate and destructive ways. For example, without ceremonies to acknowledge the tremendous changes young people undergo in adolescence, some teens act out the hero's journey with drugs, violence, and unwise sexual encounters. When a lifetime of work is not acknowledged with a rite-of-passage ritual, retired people often sicken and die earlier than they would if a passage into the next phase of their life had been celebrated.

The hero's journey map is built into our core. When children play pretend games, they instinctually have the hero, the villain, the task, the challenge, and the victory. Fairy tales tell the story of the hero's journey in which the hero is tested and finally prevails as he and his mate "live happily ever after."

There are recurring elements in a hero's journey which deserve a bit more detail. (See the Wheel of the Hero's Journey in Part Four.) Each journey does not necessarily contain all of these elements, but the trial-victory model is constant. You can find this story in myth and fairy tales, but it is also the story of you as you live through the seasons and changes of your life; that is why it is more powerful with every retelling and variation. Whether the story comes from our own life, whether it is told in a ritual, or whether the story is told in myth or fairy tale, the elements are the same.

Every hero's story begins with a subtle shift in ordinary energy, sometimes called the "winds of change." You may be at home minding your own business when the winds of change come, either as a gentle breeze or a gale. You feel an imminent shift in your life, but you may not know what the shift will be about. For example, before babies make a behavioral shift into the next level of mobility (e.g., crawling, standing, or walking), they often go through a time of great frustration, as if they know a change is coming but they are not quite ready for it. As an adult, you may feel when a shift in your career is coming; you may feel excitement or trepidation before you even know what the change will entail. At this point you have the choice to resist the coming change, but not without risking metaphorical or literal maladies.

Soon enough you make a commitment to the journey. You set sail on the "river of no return," meaning that you can no longer be the same person you were before you began; you will either go back to your metaphorical home in defeat, having not met the challenge, or you will complete the hero's journey and come back changed and victorious. In myth and fairy tale, this moment occurs when the hero accepts the challenge handed to him. Hercules goes out in search of the golden fleece; a lover sets his sights on his future bride; the homeowner signs the contract.

As the hero's journey is accepted, the real work—struggle, growth, and transformation—begins. During this time of struggle, you become the person who will ultimately be victorious in your challenge. This is the time when you study for years to get a degree; it is the time in therapy when you tell your deepest truth; it is the time in modern vision quests when the seeker is alone in the desert; it is the time in tribal initiatory rituals when the young people are surviving in the wilderness.

During this time of struggle in the hero's journey, you are sometimes assisted by a helper. In tribal initiatory practices that involve hallucinogens, a helper could appear as an animal totem in a dream. In the fairy tale of Snow White, she has the help of the seven dwarves. In the wedding ceremony, the maid of honor, the best man and the other attendants are the symbolic helpers of the couple that is taking on the hero's challenge of marriage.

You are often set face-to-face with a foe during this time of struggle in the hero's journey, an actual or symbolic energy that works against you. Although you root for the hero and rail against the villain, the foe is actually a sacred helper. You must grow yourself stronger, wiser, and more powerful than the foe. In this way, your enemy is your greatest friend, because he forces you to become the new person who triumphs. In order to understand how essential the energy of the foe is, think of the Exodus from Egypt without the Pharaoh, or the Jesus story without Judas. These archetypical stories would not be rooted in our collective psyche were it not for the formidable energy of the enemy that must be overcome. We need our foes to live the hero's story. Our enemies become our sacred allies as we grow on our way to becoming heroes.

In ritual, the foe often appears as a symbolic resistance, an effort to keep the hero from moving forward. In tribal initiatory ceremonies, the mothers hold onto their sons and cry as the men of the tribe pull them from their mothers' arms and into the ritual that will make them men. In the Ritual of a Woman's Wisdom Time, the young women hold onto the woman who is celebrating menopause, until she breaks free and joins her sisters on the other side of the portal.

The moment of transformation, that instant when the old is left behind and the new is embraced, is often symbolized in ritual by moving through a portal, such as when the bride is carried across the threshold, leaving the world of maidenhood behind and emerging as a wife. In myth and fairy tale the transformative moment is symbolized by death and rebirth, as when Sleeping Beauty wakes to true love's kiss or the phoenix rises from the ashes of its own death. In religious stories the transformation of the hero is resurrection, as in the rising up of Innana, Persephone, and Jesus. In every case the hero is made into a new being by his or her own struggle and surrender to the process of transformation.

Heroes often receive a gift as they transform, as an outward symbol of the inward change. Wedding rings, diplomas, retirement watches, and stars on arithmetic papers are examples of gifts that celebrate the victorious transition to a new life. Virtually any happy ending to any story, movie, or life passage involves some gift, whether it be a present, a sincerely expressed appreciation, or a good feeling inside. The gift signifies that a change has taken place.

In ritual, giving a gift as part of the culmination of the ceremony deepens the experience of the entire passage. (Refer to the chapter "Use of Symbols.") Almost anything can be used as a symbol if it is presented in the context of the ritual. For example, a piece of bone can symbolize the wisdom of the ancestors; a pinch of dried herb can symbolize healing energy; a drop of water can symbolize the purification of body, mind, and spirit; the passing of a flame can symbolize transference of power. I have kept a thimble-sized piece of charred wood on my altar for years symbolizing my walk across burning coals. It is the meaning we place on these objects that make them suitable gifts for the culmination of a hero's journey.

After the great adventure, the hero goes back home to everyday life. Of course, the hero is changed forever, but regular time, space, and the normal flow of energy continue until it is time for the next hero's journey. Frodo returns home at the end of the ring trilogy; the gods and goddesses return to Mt. Olympus after running around on earth with the humans; Han Solo and Princess Leia return to their lives after they have saved the Federation; the graduate goes home after the party. The return to a normal existence can be summed up in the well-known ending: "And they lived happily ever after."

At different stages of your life, it is appropriate to celebrate major changes by viewing them as hero's journeys and deepening them with ritual. Referring to the Wheel of a Lifetime in Part Four, note that the wheel can symbolize not only a year, but an entire lifetime. Each stage of your life can be placed on all the Wheels in Part Four. Your conception is the moment of the birth of light, the place on the wheel where we find the winter solstice. Your childhood is in the East, or in spring-time. Your sexual maturity comes about when spring's arrival is celebrated, three-eighths of the way around the circle. Marriage is in the South, in the month of June, as well as your active adult years. The harvest time on the calendar corresponds to the reaching of goals in your later adult life, which ultimately leads to old age and retirement. The holiday for the dead (Halloween, or Samhain) is on the circle where you enter our own transition from this life, leading to the time referred to as "rest." Then the cycle begins again.

Each stage of your life holds the potential to make the journey heroic, sacred, and conscious. This section of the book contains rituals for each stage of life.

. *Baby Blessing* .

The Baby Blessing can be used in place of or in addition to a religious ceremony, such as a christening. This ritual uses an officiant, but a non-clergy person may also be appropriate. Extended family and friends may participate, or an intimate celebration with just the parents and the baby may be what is desired. If there is no officiant, the parents may take turns reading the parts that the officiant would speak. In place of responding to the vows, the parents may simply discuss their parenting promises.

Materials:

A table for an altar

A container of water

A rose or other sweet-smelling flower

A candle

A container of maple syrup

Set up:

Create an altar with the items listed above.

Have family and friends assembled in front of the altar.

The baby rests in the arms of a parent.

As the parents step forward holding the baby, the officiant begins.

☦

Officiant: "Welcome, beloved ones. We are here to celebrate the gift of life. This little one in our midst embodies the miracle of life we celebrate today. As we celebrate this miracle, we also realize that this baby's presence—so new and perfect—reminds us that the same perfect life is in each one of us. We recognize this child as an immortal being clothed in flesh who has chosen, in some mysterious way, to come to this world to bless us. We recognize this being as a mature soul within this small, sweet body, yet we are not deceived by its appearance of newness; this child is wise, unique, whole, and purposeful right now.

"Our intention here today is to recognize this child's perfection, to welcome the child to earth and into our midst, and to pledge, along with its family, to see this child for the unrepeatable miracle that he is now, and the miracle that he becomes as he grows into a child, an adolescent, a young adult, and on, for as long as we are blessed with his company. It is so easy to see this little one as perfect and divine. We have the opportunity to remind ourselves that the same perfect and divine life that we see in this baby is in us as well.

"Additionally, we are here to witness the promises of parenthood that [*parents' names*] will make in support of each other and their child. Although the mystery of new life has already made them parents, we witness and celebrate their conscious acceptance of that sacred state of parenthood."

Officiant: "[*Parents' names*], you have been given the gift of parenthood. All of us here bless you and thank you for making the selfless decision to give of your energy, your time, your resources, and mostly, your love, to nurture this being of light. May the joys of parenthood overshadow any sleepless night, stress, or challenge that you may experience in the days and years to come as parents of this precious baby. Know that all of us here today support you and are here for you as you find your way as a family together. In order to make this day even more significant, I have some questions for you to answer in the presence of these people, who love you and love your baby.

"Do you believe that you have been given an incomparable gift by being made into the parents of this babe?"

Parents: "We do."

Officiant: "Will you teach this child the highest truths of life as purely as you understand them, always striving to become wiser, more patient, and more loving yourselves?"

Parents: "We will."

Officiant: : "Will you always love and respect the uniqueness of the life that springs forth from your child as a spiritual person with a purpose and a mission on earth?"

Parents: "We will."

Officiant: "Will you conduct your own lives as examples to your child of divine qualities in action, among which are love, peace, joy, and harmony?"

Parents: "We will."

Officiant: "And finally, do you promise to nurture your own relationship so that you may be a harbor of contentment for each other, and that your home may be a sanctuary for yourselves and your child?"

Parents: "We do."

Officiant: "And so, [*parents' names*], as we all live in the company of each other going forward through the years, you will not only be known as [*parents' names*], you will also be known as [*Here use the names that the parents will be referred to by the child, such as 'Mommy' and 'Dad'*] of this child. *(Gentle applause.)* What name have you chosen for your child?"

Parents respond with the baby's full name.

Officiant: "[*Baby's name*], let us celebrate the earthly elements of life with you as a way of welcoming you to this earth and as a symbol of all the delights we wish for you in your life here. The gifts of water, air, fire, and earth are what our bodies are made of and what this realm offers in so many wondrous ways."

The family goes to the altar, and the officiant offers the container of water to the baby. If the baby is six months old or younger, the parents can dip their own hands in the water and put some drops on the baby's head, hands, feet, and heart. If the baby is older than six months, the parents can encourage the baby to put its own hands in the water. Have the small towel handy.

Officiant: "Water is the element of purification and nonresistance. With it, we celebrate your purity. Our wish for you is that your life always flows in powerful ways."

The officiant offers the rose for the baby to smell.

Officiant: "May the breath of God fill your body with great health and your mind with wonderful ideas."

The officiant shows the baby the lighted candle.

Officiant: "The flame of passion is in your spirit; we wish for you that you accomplish all you came to do on earth. We are all here to help you."

The officiant offers the container of maple syrup. A parent can put a finger into the syrup and then into the baby's mouth, or a tiny spoon may be used.

Officiant: "This sweet syrup is made from earth, sunlight, and the wisdom of the maple tree. It symbolizes the sweetness of life that we all wish for you. It also symbolizes the strength of the earth that makes up your bones and the intelligence that is found in all of nature, including you."

If the officiant is comfortable holding the baby, he or she now takes the child. Otherwise, the baby can be addressed while still in the arms of its parent.

Officiant: "Dearest [*child's name*], we see you for the perfect expression of life that you are. Thank you for coming to bless us. Whether we are aware of it or not, we have been waiting for you. You are here now, and we are so very happy. Our life is expanded and blessed because of you. We know you have great work to do, and we are here to support you. You are a miracle; you are magnificent; you are capable of all that you came to accomplish. By our seeing who you truly are, may you be reminded of the life that lives within you."

A prayer may be said to conclude this ritual, or the officiant may say the following:

Officiant: "As we have truly seen this holy child, may we take a moment and look into each others' faces and truly see each other. We are each unrepeatable miracles who have come to earth with purpose and mission. May we empower each other and ourselves by seeing those who, in this moment, see us. As [*parents' names*] have vowed to care for and nurture [*child's name*], may we know that we are nurtured by the power of life. As [*child's name*] is now enfolded in the arms of his parent, may we know that we are forever enfolded in the loving embrace of our creator. Blessed be."

Maiden Ceremony

The Maiden Ceremony initiates girls who have started their menses into the community of women. As significant as it is for the girls, it is even more powerful for the adult women, most of whom were not celebrated as they passed this milestone in their growing up. This version of the Maiden Ceremony is for a group of girls and women, but could be adjusted for a single family.

Since this ceremony so completely celebrates the feminine, I've used the word "goddess" to identify that aspect of God, though another word may be used if the participants so choose.

Materials:

A draped chair for each girl

A garland for each girl's head, made by her mother

A small clamshell with a pearl glued inside for each girl

Other gifts as desired

Flowers for a sacred circle

Set up:

Drape and arrange the chairs in a row in front of the room.

Arrange the gifts on an altar.

Have the mothers of the maidens stand behind each chair with the garlands they have made for their daughters.

Create a sacred circle of flowers around the group of chairs.

Prepare a feast and have it ready in an adjacent room or space.

Several women can lead different sections of the ritual, or the entire ritual can be led by the same woman. As the ceremony begins, the participants are seated and the maidens, blindfolded, are each led in by an adult woman. Stopping just outside of the circle, they wait while the women sing a welcoming song or chant.

✚

Leader: "Maidens, welcome to the circle of women. You may remove your blind-folds."

They do, but remain outside the sacred circle.

Leader: "Today is a life-changing day for you because today you leave your child-hood behind and enter the era of your life known as maidenhood. Your initiation into maidenhood has already been accomplished by the goddess who gave you the gift of your first blood flow, but today is your celebration, acknowledging the miracle of that change and your entry into the circle of women. Before you step into the women's circle, symbolized by the ring of flowers, I ask you, what is it you are leaving behind?"

The girls, who should have been given this question to think about prior to the ceremony, answer with such statements as "I leave behind making excuses for my behavior," or "I leave behind my anger at my little brother," or "I leave behind hiding candy in my room." When each has responded, the leader or another woman continues.

Leader: "Good. You may find that other things naturally fall away as you step into the powerful era of maidenhood. Now, acknowledging each of you as a young maiden, precious to us and the goddess, transformed from the little girl that you were, we ask you to step over the line of flowers and enter the circle where your mothers await you. Please sit in the chair in front of your mother."

They do.

Leader: "I now invite the mothers to present their daughters to this assembly of women and place the garland made for them on their head. Please, mothers, tell us about your precious maidens, that we may celebrate each young woman with you."

The mothers introduce their daughters, briefly tell what they love and honor about them, and crown them with the garland they made for them.

Leader: "Traditionally older women have taught younger women about the mysteries of womanhood. Although the sacredness of the blood mysteries has been largely lost, today we share those mysteries with you and hope that you will share them with your daughters in the future.

"When a girl has attained the age that you have, her womb matures and begins to flow with blood in a monthly cycle that will last, for most women, approximately forty years. We call it your 'moon time' because it used to be that, when humans lived in rhythm with nature, women's blood flowed with the full moon; all women of childbearing age in a village or tribe flowed at the same time, with the phases of the moon. The blood is sacred because it provides nourishment for a fertilized egg when a baby is started. Though we expect it will be many years before any of you begin growing a baby in your womb, your body is ready, and every month much of your body's energy is spent in preparing a possible home for a new life. When a baby is not started, your blood flows out and, as such, is the only blood in nature that is freely given and not taken in bloodshed. It represents the woman's ability to give life and is one of the sacred blessings of being born a girl.

"In the deep, dark center of your female body is the doorway between the worlds. This is the mystery. A soul enters this world through the doorway in the center of your womb. As women, we are the altars into which new life comes and in which the souls of the next generation clothe themselves in flesh. Your body is sacred, and you should always regard it as such. It is our prayer that you will never give your body to another out of fear, desperation, peer pressure, or force. It is our prayer that, when the time comes, you give your body in total reverence and love for yourself and your partner.

"Our gift for you today is this shell with a pearl inside. *(She gives a shell and pearl to each maiden.)* The shell represents your mature womb, open to the possibility of new life. The pearl represents the beginning of new life in it. Our heartfelt wish for each of you is that every egg fertilized in the doorway at the center of your being be the beginning of a baby who is deeply desired and conceived in love.

"Your moon time represents a wonderful rhythm for your life. When you are bleeding it is natural to want to be less active, more introspective, and more to yourself. In our modern culture many women achieve this rest for themselves by creating menstrual cramps and emotional outbursts. Ancient people knew that a woman's bleeding time was a sacred time of rest and reju-venation. At those times the women of the village would go to a special tent or hut and be waited on by the girls and older women. It was believed that the bleeding women were particularly intuitive, and sometimes decisions that affected the entire culture were left to the women in the tent. Let your own rhythm lead you in your cycles. If more introspection feels right to you, give that to yourself. You do not need to create illness for yourself in order to honor your body's natural rhythm.

"At the end of your childbearing years another mystery occurs; your blood stops flowing. Just as the beginning of your moon times is not honored in the larger world today, the entry into the wisdom time of life is not respected for the mystery that it represents, either. After forty years of a woman's body being available for the creation of new people, and much energy being spent each month for that readiness, the doorway is closed. Instead of a woman bleeding each month, a woman begins retaining her blood when she reaches fifty or so years. No longer is her bodily energy directed toward the creation of new life; it is carried within her, and she may direct it toward all of humanity.

"Today a woman has many productive years after she turns fifty—almost half her life. In her matriarch years, after she stops bleeding and before she reaches her elder years, a woman has more time, energy, and wisdom to give to the world. May it be for you, maidens, that after your years of bleeding, falling in love, partnering, and bringing new life (if it is your choice and the goddess grants you the gift of babies), that you have many years to give your energy, wisdom, and love to the world.

"However, today that time is far, far off. Today we honor the beginning of bleeding in your young lives. You have much to learn and many adventures to look forward to in the years ahead. Like our ancestors did in the past, I now ask you to open yourselves to the advice of these women who love you and who have lived through many of the experiences that you are headed for. *(Speaking to the assembled women who have been witnesses up to this point.)* Women, what advice do you have for these maidens?"

The adult women may shout out advice, such as "Don't be afraid to take risks," and "Let your communication be clear and powerful," and "Be silly," and "Remember to dance," and "Always tell yourself the truth." If these ceremonies happen regularly, it is useful to publish these tidbits of advice from previous ceremonies for the maidens in the current group. When the advice winds down, the leader or another woman continues, speaking now to the maidens' mothers.

Leader: "Mothers of these beautiful maidens, it is appropriate for all of us to honor you today also. It was the doorway in your bodies that opened for these wondrous beings to move through into this life. It was your bodies that nurtured their bodies. It was your homes that nurtured their souls, your days and weeks and years that were given in service to their expression. It was your love and wisdom that has already seen them through joys and hardships. May your joy today be full. Let us honor you."

All women applaud the mothers or sing them a song.

Leader: "Maidens, all of the women around you—your mothers, grandmothers, and friends—honor you and welcome you to womanhood. May the world grow more peaceful through your feminine love and service. May women and men, alike, grow more forgiving, more generous, and more selfless because you are in the world. May beauty flourish; may joy abound; may love grow because you chose to come to earth. Let us all now honor you.

All women applaud the maidens or sing them a song.

Leader: "We will let your mothers have a moment with you now as we prepare the Angel Walk to the feast in your honor."

The mothers share a moment of love with their daughters, perhaps giving them a special gift.

For the Angel Walk, the assembled women form two lines with a narrow corridor running down the middle leading toward the meal. The mothers place the blindfolds on their daughters and direct them to the rows of women. The maidens are then handed, woman by woman, down the opening between the two lines. As the maidens pass through the corridor, the women whisper words of love, empowerment, and truth to them. For example, "You are a treasure,"

"Thank you for coming to earth," "You are a miracle," and "You are so strong; there is nothing you cannot accomplish." The Angel Walk can be quite powerful and a bit disorienting for the maidens. The mothers should be ready to receive them when they are handed out of the corridor at the other end. Remove their blindfolds; give them a warm hug and everyone enjoy a great meal.

. Coming of Age for Boys .

The Coming of Age for Boys ritual initiates boys into the circle of men. Unlike girls who become women at a specific time, boys have no such biological marker. The age for boys entering manhood is around the age of twelve or thirteen, perhaps the time of middle or junior high school, or whenever the boy is ready to accept greater responsibility and move away from the lifestyle of a young child. At this time, boys may begin taking a sexual interest in their bodies; some may develop more complex bonds with their parents. Because there are so few positive pathways for boys to become men in our culture, it is important to provide them a healthy portal into manhood so that they do not create it for themselves in dangerous or antisocial ways.

This ritual can encompass an entire weekend with the ceremonial components spread over two or more nights, or it can be accomplished in one overnight time frame. A wilderness experience, such as a long hike, a rock climb, a sea or lake passage, a ropes course or elements of a vision quest, give the ritual even more power. The men and boys might also build something together as part of the journey to manhood.

Our entire culture benefits when its boys receive training and acknowledgment in becoming strong, wise, balanced men. This ceremony takes the place of great initiatory ordeals, filled with danger and requiring great courage and stamina, which were a part of tribal life the world over and are still a part of our psyche today.

Materials:

    Drums

    A talking stick

    A ceremonial knife for each boy

    A journal and writing instrument for each boy

    Other gifts as desired

Set up:

    Prepare a bonfire in the country, woods, or in a fireplace.

    At another location, women should prepare a meal.

*I*n this ritual each boy is accompanied by his father or a man representing his father. Other men may participate as well, such as grandfathers and younger twenty-something men from the community or family. The boys sit together near the fire with their journals handy; the young men sit across the fire from the boys. The elders, the fathers, and grandfathers sit behind the young men and a bit higher as the wisdom keepers and witnesses. Drumming in unison begins and continues for several minutes. Then an Elder begins to speak.

☧

Elder: "Boys, welcome to the circle of men. Tonight is a life-changing time for you because it is the time that you leave your childhood behind and take on the beginning of adult responsibility and power. After tonight you will be seen as young men; may you be worthy of this change.

"Here with you are your fathers, grandfathers, older brothers, and other men who are important to you; we are here to honor you and witness this transition. The young men sitting across the fire from you will be your guides and advisors as you take this step into manhood. They are closer to your age and have recently made this transition themselves. Your fathers and grandfathers will watch the proceedings carefully, advise when necessary, and direct the ceremony.

"Becoming a man means stepping into greater wisdom, more self-discipline, and authentic power born of honesty, responsibility, and skill. Tonight we will give you what wisdom we have and hope that you will use it to make yourselves great men for the world and for yourselves in the years to come. So, we are ready to begin."

The Elder hands the talking stick to one of the young men in their twenties.

Elder: "Here is the talking stick. Speak to them of being peaceful warriors."

The young men speak one at time, passing the talking stick to the next person as they finish. They speak from their hearts about personal responsibility, honesty, developing a moral compass, the value of conscience, refraining from antisocial behavior, doing their best, having life goals, being law abiding, and handling disagreements without violence. They speak from their experience and include positive, wise advice as well as personal stories of their own struggles. When all have spoken, the Elders add anything they wish, also using the talking stick. Then the leading Elder speaks.

Elder: "You have heard our wisdom about being a peaceful warrior. Now search your hearts and discern what promises you are ready to make concerning this matter as you make the journey into manhood."

The boys ponder what they have heard and make any notes they wish in their journals.

Elder: "Speak to them of work and financial responsibility."

The young men speak about the satisfaction of doing work that one loves, about the discipline of being orderly with money, and of their personal experiences with first bank accounts, bill paying, and struggles with money management and prioritizing. They speak about the importance of having a spending plan, savings, and financial records. They speak about the good that money can do when it follows wise choices. The Elders add any advice they wish. Then the leading Elder asks the boys to think about what promises they would feel good about making concerning their handling of money and work responsibilities. The boys take a moment to do this and write any notes they wish in their journals.

Elder: "Speak to them of friendship."

The young men speak about the importance of nurturing friendships and being a good friend. They speak about the value of teamwork and trust, loyalty and common values. They share about the pitfalls of peer pressure and the importance of finding friends with similar positive values. As before, the Elders add any wisdom they wish; the boys contemplate their potential promises about this subject and make their notes.

Elder: "Speak to them about the health of their body, mind, and spirit."

The young men share their thoughts and feelings about making wise decisions to keep their bodies healthy and vital, about mental health and how they can contribute to their own mental well-being, and about following a spiritual practice which serves their soul. They talk about a balanced life and how important it is to nurture themselves in all these areas so they will be the best they can be for themselves, their families, and the world. They speak of the destructive influence of harmful substances and how difficult it is to break an addiction. As before, personal sharing of struggles in the area of self-care is valuable. The Elders contribute their wis-

dom, and the boys think about how they will commit to this area of manhood.

Elder: "Now speak to them of sexuality and love."

The young men speak about their own first experiences of sexual attraction. They speak about the importance of honesty and mutual respect when love happens. They speak about the common threads of friendship skills and relationship skills. They speak about birth control and honoring a "no" in their own hearts or from their partner. They can share about what they first looked for in a partner and what they value now as young adult men. As with each of these categories, love can be a subject with a great lack of clarity; the young men can share their uncertainties and confusion about love as they have shared their struggles about the previous subjects. They share about how the boys' relationships with their mothers and siblings will change because of this ceremony. When the young men finish, the Elders share their wisdom. The boys think this over and discern any commitments they feel comfortable about making.

Elder: "You have heard our wisdom, and you have heard our uncertainties about the places in our lives that are still growing. May we always continue to grow wiser. Boys, tomorrow morning you will be asked to speak your covenant of manhood. Consider what you have heard, what you know, and what you aspire to be. Remember that as you speak your covenant and make your promises, all of us here are supporting you to keep your word and to become the men you were born to be. We meet again in the morning."

Drumming closes the assembly. The boys spend a good part of the night carefully crafting the set of promises that will usher them into manhood.

In the morning they all assemble again, the boys sitting on one side of the fire or ceremonial space and the young men and Elders on the other side. Drumming opens the morning. If outdoor activities are planned for this day, such as a hike or a physical ordeal of any kind, the ritual would continue in the evening. The leading Elder opens the ceremony.

Elder: "It is the time that you boys enter your time of manhood. This is the moment after which there is no turning back. This is the time to make promises about the kind of man you will be, beginning with the next breath you take after stepping to the side of the men. Your family here—your father, your grandfather, your older brother, or the man who honors you in the role of your elder—has a present for you to commemorate this passage. It is a knife. A knife has similar energy to that of a man. Both knife and man can define, create, provide, protect, and master the world around him. A knife and a man can also destroy, not only that which should be destroyed to make room for something new, but also that which is precious. This knife is given to remind you that, with every choice you make in life, you use your energy for life-giving endeavors or life-draining destruction. Use your knife well, as you wisely use every day of your life as a man.

"Who is the first boy to become a man?"

The first boy stands and reads or speaks his covenant. When he is finished, his grandfather or the oldest man supporting this particular boy stands with the knife. He introduces his boy to the group, telling everyone the wonderful qualities of this young person and affirming his readiness to become a man. The next oldest man, knowing this particular boy, also speaks about him and his admirable qualities. This proceeds until all who know this boy intimately have spoken.

Then the man who is most closely related to the boy, probably his father, stands in front of his son with the knife. He speaks of his pride in witnessing his son take this passage. With the side of the knife he touches the boy's forehead and says, "May you be blessed with great visionary thoughts." He touches the boy's lips with the side of the knife and says, "May your words always express the truth that frees and empowers." He touches the boy's heart and says, "May your heart be filled with passion and courage." Then he lays the knife in his son's hands and says, "May the work of your hands bless the world and make you fulfilled. Welcome to the circle of men." The boy crosses over to the side of the men and is honored with drum beats.

This process continues until all the boys have all crossed over to the side of the men. The leading Elder speaks, addressing the new initiates.

Elder: "Men, we honor you and welcome you to the circle of men. We are here to support you in living your covenant and deepening your desire to live your purpose on earth. May the world be more peaceful because you are here. May those people whose lives you touch feel safer, more generous of heart, and more connected with each other because you express all that you are. We, those of us who have known you from birth, receive you as the gifts to the world that you are."

The men then close the circle again by filling in where the boys had been. They drum and chant.

Men: "We honor you. We empower you to be who you are."

The men pack up and return to the home where the women have prepared the feast. At this gathering of the families, the initiates once again read or speak their covenants. The women of the family, the mothers, grandmothers, and sisters, speak their promises to their special young man in a formal way, so that all assembled recognize that relationships and roles have changed with this passage. The boys have gone through their hero's journey and have returned home men, changed and ready to serve in a larger way. The women speak of seeing their son, their grandson, their brother, afresh, as a man instead of a boy. After dinner each family can speak of the new freedoms and responsibilities that form the agreement for the changed family system.

. *Birthday Ritual* .

This ritual is written as a ceremony with five or more friends of the person being celebrated. However, it can be a performed with fewer than five friends, or even alone if you like, by reading the questions and writing the answers yourself, or having a friend ask the questions from all four directions. This ritual can be a part of a larger, more traditional birthday party, or it can be experienced as its own celebration.

Material:

A birthday box—about half the size of a shoe box, decorated in a symbolic way, to be used year after year

Four small candles, yellow, red, blue, and white, that fit in the box

Matches

The Birthday Wheel and the Unfolding Year Wheel (found in Part Four)

Writing instrument

A symbol or picture of that which represents the year to come for the birthday celebrant

Set up:

Create a circle with a chair or pillow in the middle and the directions identified with the candles, the yellow for the East, red for the South, blue in the West, and white in the North.

Assign four people to sit near each of the candles. The person in the East should hold the matches, the Birthday Wheel, the Unfolding Year Wheel, and a writing instrument.

The birthday person should have decided on or created the symbol which represents the year to come in his or her life; he should have this symbol with him during the ceremony.

The friends sit around the circumference of the circle, and the person who is celebrating the birthday is invited to sit in the center.

Leader: "Dear [*name*], today represents the anniversary of the day you took your first breath on this earth. We acknowledge your soul's decision to come here, and we are so blessed to be with you today.

"Birthdays are powerful markers on our personal calendar; they offer the opportunity to review the past year and to look ahead to discern what what it is you wish to accomplish, experience, or contribute. Your friends and family, who have created this circle of love around you, are here to witness your remembrance of past accomplishments and to witness that which you call forth for the year ahead.

"In addition to your family and friends, four candles line the circumference of this circle, one for each of the four directions. Each color and direction represents different energies which you have used this past year to live your life and express your purpose. As we all participate in this birthday ritual you will tell us, and we will witness, what you have experienced and contributed this past year. There are four dear friends sitting with the four candles. They will write your thoughts on the Birthday Wheel as you answer their questions. So, dear [name], please begin by facing East and lighting the yellow candle."

Friend in the East: "Dear [name], East is the direction of the rising sun, new beginnings, and great inspiration. Tell us how the gifts of the East have blessed you since your last birthday by answering this question: What endeavors did you begin this year?"

As the birthday person answers this question, the friend in the East writes the answer in the eastern quadrant of the Birthday Wheel. When the answer and the writing are complete, the Birthday Wheel is passed to the representative of the South. The birthday person is invited to face the South and light the red candle.

Friend in the South: "Dear [*name*], the South is the direction of lavish giving. When the sun is high in the southern sky, the summer season is upon the land. Nature gives greatly to her plants in the summer so that they grow lush with life. Your life is the gift you give when you serve in the way that your soul dictates. Please answer this question, dear [*name*]: What and whom did you serve this year?"

The birthday person answers, and the representative of the South writes the answer in the southern quadrant of the Birthday Wheel. When this is complete the birthday person is invited to face the West and light the blue candle.

Friend in the West: "Dear [*name*], the West is the direction of endings and completion, just as the day ends when the sun goes down below the western horizon. Your life brought you endings this year; some may have been sad and others wonderful with dreams fulfilled and goals accomplished. Please answer this question: What did you complete this year?"

As before, the birthday person answers, and the representative of the West writes the answers in the western quadrant of the Birthday Wheel. Then the birthday person is asked to face the North and light the white candle.

Friend in the North: "Dear [*name*], the North is the direction of the ancestors. We will become the ancestors of future generations so it is important to leave a positive legacy and make the world a better place. So, dear [*name*], please answer this final question about your contributions this past year: What did you leave as a legacy?"

The birthday person answers this final question, and the notes are written in the northern quadrant of the Birthday Wheel. The leader hands the completed Birthday Wheel to the birthday person.

Leader: "Thank you, dear [*name*], for sharing the blessings and challenges of this past year. We honor you for all you are and all you give. This Birthday Wheel is yours to contemplate and use as you see fit. It is a wonderful reminder of how you have given your life. We hope you feel that your miraculous 365 days were spent for good.

"Now it is time for you to set your intentions for the coming year as we witness and bless your goals and aspirations. Once again you will be asked four questions about the coming year. After you answer each question and the writers have captured your intentions on the Unfolding Year Wheel, we ask that you blow out each candle and make a wish. Making birthday wishes by blowing out candles is an ancient tradition. Our ancestors believed that the wishes were carried on the smoke from the extinguished candles to the realm of the gods, who had the power to grant the wishes. Now, dear [*name*], once again please face the East."

Friend in the East: "Dear [*name*], the coming year is fertile with new possibilities. Please answer this question for yourself and us here who love and support you: What will you begin this year?"

The answer is written in the eastern quadrant of the Unfolding Year Wheel.

Friend in the East: "Now please blow out the yellow candle and make a wish about your new beginnings."

The birthday person does this and turns to face the South.

Friend in the South: "Dear [*name*], the energy of the coming year unconditionally supports you and your endeavors. Life yearns to serve you so that you can serve life. Please answer this question: What and who will you serve this year?"

The answer is spoken and recorded.

Friend in the South: "Please blow out the red candle and make a wish about your talents, energy, and love being well used."

This is done, and the birthday person turns to face the West.

Friend in the West: "Dear [name], the wisdom and energy of the West can help you complete what needs to be completed this coming year. Please tell us the answer to this question: What will you complete this year?"

The birthday person answers, and the friend in the West records the information.

Friend in the West: "Please blow out the blue candle, and as you do make a wish about completion or endings."

This is done, and the birthday person turns and faces North.

Friend in the North: "Dear [name], you were born on this earth with a purpose and a reason. As you give the gifts you came to give, the world becomes a better place, and you leave a legacy for our children and our children's children. Please answer this question: What will you leave to benefit future generations this year?"

The birthday person responds, and the friend in the North records the answer. The birthday person is asked to make a wish about leaving their legacy, and then he or she blows out the white candle. The leader hands the completed Unfolding Year Wheel to the birthday person.

Leader: "Dear [*name*], thank you for stating your intentions for the coming year and allowing your family and friends to witness your declarations and add our support. You hold the written account of that which you wish to accomplish this year. I encourage you to keep this document for the next year in your birthday box. A year from today, on your birthday, read over what has been recorded today. We have absolute faith in life's support of you and in your ability to accomplish all that you set forth and more.

"Finally, dear [*name*], please share your sacred symbol or picture with us, and tell how it represents the coming year for you."

The birthday person speaks of the symbol or picture which he has chosen to represent the upcoming year.

Leader: "The ceremony honoring your day of birth is almost over, but the effects of today's ritual will be felt for the entire year to come and beyond. I encourage you to keep the candles, the birthday Wheels, and your symbol tucked away in your birthday box. Think of your intentions and symbol as being planted in fertile soil. In the perfect way and in the perfect time they will be born. On your birthday next year, open the box and see what you have accomplished. Thank you, dear [name], for so consciously dedicating your life to good. We now respectfully end this ritual by closing the sacred circle as we come forward to congratulate our friend, [name]."

All the participants move forward to hug and congratulate the birthday person.

. *Driver's License Ritual* .

This ritual honors a new driver and is performed around the vehicle that the driver will usu-
ally operate, though several drivers-to-be could be honored. One car would be sufficient even
with several families and several new drivers. The circle of petals would need to be made large
enough for all drivers to get inside along with the car.

Materials:

>Sage
>A bowl of flower petals
>Gift pouch and small gifts in a covered bowl
>The vehicle

Set up:

>Position the car in a driveway or other private area with plenty of space for
>people to walk around it.

T he leader of the ritual, possibly a parent of the driver-to-be, begins by saying a
prayer for the proceedings. The driver is invited to smudge the vehicle with sage.

This is done by lighting a bunch of dried sage until it smokes but not flames, then wafting the smoke around the outside and inside the vehicle. The person holding the bowl of flower petals creates a sacred circle by scattering petals on the ground around the car, reserving a few of the petals for the end of the ritual.

✿

Leader: "Will the licensed drivers step into the sacred circle of drivers, making ourselves ready to admit a new one into our circle?"

The licensed drivers step into the sacred circle with the leader and the vehicle.

Charge to the driver-to-be, spoken by the leader from inside the circle: "By moving into this level of adulthood represented by a driver's license, you accept great freedom and responsibility. [*Driver's name*], do you promise to always follow the rules of the road when you are driving?"

Driver: "I do."

Leader: "Do you promise to have safety first in your mind above all else while you are driving or riding?"

Driver: "I do."

Leader: "Do you promise to notify family of your whereabouts, or change in plans or schedule, when not doing so could lead to worry and concern?"

Driver: "I do."

Leader: "Do you promise to maintain your car as a safe vehicle?"

Driver: "I do."

Leader: "Repeat after me: *(Leader speaks the following in short phrases allowing the driver to repeat them.)* 'I vow to conduct myself as a safe driver all the years that I drive. I promise to have my safety always in mind, as well as the safety of my passengers, other drivers, pedestrians, animals, and property around me. I promise to never alter my ability to drive safely with alcohol or chemicals. If I ever feel unsafe to drive, I will call or ask for help. I will neither participate in, nor allow others in any car in which I am driving or riding to participate in dangerous or foolish behavior. If I find myself in such a situation, I promise to leave and call for assistance. As I do everything I can to promote my own safety, I then trust in God as my ultimate safety.'"

Uncover the gift pouch and gifts. Everyone who wishes to give the new driver-to-be gifts do so with a statement of their hopes for the future. The gifts should be small enough so they all fit into the pouch; the pouch, in turn, should be small enough to fit into the glove box of any vehicle. Gifts might include a road assistance card, a twenty dollar bill for an emergency, a personal totem or charm for safety, a photo of loved ones, written blessings, or an extra house key.

Leader: "May you carry these tokens of love and good wishes in the glove box of every car you drive for your lifetime. When you see the pouch, remember this experience here today and how deeply you are loved. May your driving years be filled with joy, exploration, and safety."

The licensed drivers position themselves at the driver's open door and make a passageway for the new driver to enter the car.

Leader: "In anticipation of passing your driver's test tomorrow and receiving your driver's license, we now invite you into the sacred circle of drivers."

The children in the celebration (the non-drivers) send the young driver into the circle and into the driver's seat of the car. The leader sprinkles the remainder of the flower petals on the hood of the car above the seated driver-to-be. Everyone cheers. After the driver's test, preferably the following day, a final acknowledgment with balloons welcoming the official driver home concludes the ritual.

. *Graduation* .

Though this ritual honors those graduating from high school, it can be adapted for any person or group of people moving through a passage of scholarly accomplishment. This ritual is written for a group of friends who are graduating together and their families who have watched each other's children grow up. It could be adapted for a single graduate with many family members and friends or a single graduate celebrating with his own family.

Materials:

One river stone (approximately one-inch diameter) for each graduate

One river stone for each adult or family member to have one for each graduate *(For example, for 10 adults and 6 graduates, you will need 66 stones.)*

A clear plastic or glass saucer large enough for all the stones of the graduate to be layered in

Clear resin mixture from a craft store

Permanent fine point markers of various colors

A cloth pouch for each graduate

Set up:

Arrange stones, pouches, and pens on the altar or table.

*A*s the families arrive, the leader takes the non-graduating participants aside, asking them to search their heart and think of the one word that best expresses the sentiment they wish for each graduate. The leader then gives them a stone for each graduate and asks them to write their word on the stone, keeping the stone with them or placing it in a private place where it can dry and not become smudged.

Each graduate is asked to write his or her name on a stone and to place the stone in a secure place as well.

When it is time for the ceremony, the graduates are gathered together and the non-graduates sit facing them. One person may lead the entire ceremony or each part may be taken by a different leader.

✦

Leader: "It has been such a joy for all of us here to watch you grow and develop into the magnificent young adults that you are today. We have been blessed to have you, each and every one, in our homes and in our lives. We are now nearly finished raising you, and the changes and adjustments you make in your lives will, from now on, be attributed to your own decisions. We have endeavored to give you life skills over the years; some life skills you have learned because of our efforts and some life skills you have learned in spite of our efforts. As you graduate and move into the next phase of your lives, we acknowledge that we will not be together as we have been over the years.

Because not all of us here know the plans of each of you, would you each share with us what the next era of your life holds?"

The graduates each respond.

Leader: "Each of us here honors all that you have accomplished in your lives thus far, and we are so proud of you for who you are and what you plan to do with your lives. We have a deep desire for your happiness and success, and we want to take this opportunity to bless your endeavors. Here is a pouch which will hold our wishes for you as this ceremony progresses."

The leader hands each graduate an empty pouch and asks him or her to put his or her name stone in the pouch.

Leader: "Although each of us can claim only one of you as our blood, we all claim each of you as extended family. We see you all as very important people in each others' lives. We want you to know that any of you can come to any of us for any reason for the rest of our lives. Our support of you knows no bounds. Now each of us has a wish for you, which we ask you to accept and place in your pouches as a symbol of all the love and support that we have in our hearts for you."

The participants present their stones to the graduates and speak for a bit about why they chose their particular word as their gift.

Leader: "We want these wishes to nurture you in times to come. As you each go forth into the next phase of your lives, there will be challenges as well as joys. These gifts that you have been given represent our love for you and the qualities that are available to you from life in every moment. We wish to create an object for you that will enable you to remember these gifts whenever you need them in the future. We also hope this object will also remind you of the people here today who love you. Please hand me back your pouches for a short time, and I will create this gift for you."

The pouches with the stones are handed back to the leader.

Leader: "Thank you for participating in this ceremony. May all the wishes shared with you become a reality in your lives in surprising and fulfilling ways, and may your own dreams for your life guide you in paths of powerful expression."

The celebratory meal is served.

To make the gifts, arrange each set of stones on a clear saucer or dish with the words written on the stone facing up and visible. Mix the resin material according to directions on the product, and pour the mixture over the stones all the way to the top of the edge of the saucer so that the filled saucer becomes a coaster. Let it dry on a level surface.

After 24 hours the coasters should be completely dry. Put them back into the pouches and send them to the graduates.

. *New Pet Ritual* .

This ritual is written for a family that is acquiring a new pet. It provides a conscious way to set intentions about the way the new pet will be integrated into the household. A special section of vows is included for families in which a child or children will have the responsibility of taking care of the pet. If the quoted script seems too formal for your family, simply use it as a guide for the themes of the ritual. If you are a single person who is creating a family with a new pet, you may accomplish all the parts to the ritual with just yourself and your new companion.

Materials:

    A bed for the new pet and symbolic items of your choice such as a candle, photos, collar, and special toys

    Important papers about pet care

    Water bowl

    A document of pet care responsibilities (if children are involved)

    A Pet Box decorated in a symbolic way

    Diary or journal book that will fit inside the Pet Box

Set up:

    Create an altar at the sleeping space for the new pet.

Fill the pet's water bowl with water.

Assign the role of leader and scribe.

Gather the family around the place where the new pet will sleep, and create an altar with items such as a pet bed, a leash, toys, a collar, a brush, or anything else that symbolizes the atmosphere and feeling you wish to create for your new pet. You might also include items such as candles or photos of other pets the family has loved.

One family member or parent acts as the leader for this part of the ritual.

✛

Leader: "Before we bring our beloved new pet into our family we create a sacred space for it. This will be its spot, and so we bless this place with our love and our intentions. We also bless the items that our pet will need for its health, comfort, and joy. I light this candle to signify that our ritual of welcoming and blessing is started."

The leader lights the candle.

Another family member or parent holds the journal in which will be written the intentions and blessings spoken by the family members.

Leader: "Everyone who has brought an article or symbol to this place, please tell us what it means and why you hold it as significant on behalf of our new pet."

For example, your pet will feel comfort and love when you brush it, so you might bless the pet's brush with the words "comfort" and "love" when placing it on the altar. As you say these words of blessing, the scribe should write them in the pet's journal. This creation of the altar with objects and the recording of the blessing qualities continue until everyone is complete.

The leading adult or parent now takes the water dish and continues.

Leader: "I'm going to pass around our pet's water dish, and each one of us will imagine that the happy qualities that we have spoken are being poured into the water. I'm going to ask [*scribe's name*] to read all the qualities we named when building the altar as we pass around the water dish."

This is done.

Leader: "We will now bless all the places that will be important for our pet; we'll sprinkle this water wherever we feel that a special blessing is needed."

The family sprinkles the water on the pet's bed, near the food bowl, in the yard, in the car, wherever the family anticipates that the new pet will spend significant time.

The leading adult or parent then takes the Pet Box and continues.

Leader: "This box will be an important part of our pet's support system, so we now bless this box, as well."

The box is sprinkled with the water. Together the family can decide what goes in the Pet Box. Veterinary information, a first photo of the pet, the diary or journal of the pet's developmental milestones, training records, phone numbers of friends and family, the children's vows, if applicable, and the qualities claimed from the first part of this ritual could all go in the Pet Box.

Children's Vows for a New Pet

If children will be responsible for the care of the pet, the parent who has the role of leader continues.

Leader: "[*Names of children*], you are about to take on the big responsibility for the care and feeding of our new pet. This is an extremely important task because you will hold the life of a special animal in your care. Its health and well-being depend on you. Are you ready to take on this important responsibility?"

The children answer affirmatively.

Leader: "In order to impress upon you the importance of this agreement I would like you to make promises that the whole family will witness. They will be written in the pet journal and will be kept in the official Pet Box forever. Are you willing to make these promises?"

Again, the children answer affirmatively. The family should decide on what responsibilities the children will hold and formulate them into questions and vows to be recorded in the pet journal. The following is one example.

Parent: "Do you promise to keep fresh water and the proper amount of food available for our pet?"

Children: "I do."

Parent: "Do you promise to exercise and groom our pet so that it will remain healthy and comfortable?"

Children: "I do."

Parent: "Do you promise to help train it with utmost consistency and kindness so that our pet will always be happy and a pleasure to us?"

Children: "I do."

Parent: "Do you promise to clean up after our pet on a daily basis and keep its dishes and bed clean and orderly?"

Children: "I do."

Parent: "Good, now repeat after me: *(Offer a phrase at a time so that repeating is easy and the meaning understandable.)* I promise to love and care for our pet with complete dedication. I know caring for our pet is an important responsibility. I will learn to listen to our pet so that I can help fulfill its needs. I will do my part to give our pet a good life. I will encourage its happiness in every way so that we will have a long and fun life together.

"Well done. You are now caretakers of our new pet. Your promises are written in the pet journal and will be kept in the Pet Box. In the years to come may you look back on these promises to see how well you learned the skills of taking care of another life."

Pet Naming Ceremony

When the pet is brought home, the whole family gathers with the new pet in one of the pet's special places that was sprinkled with the water. Everyone sits in a circle on the ground with the pet in the center of the circle. Have the water dish filled and the journal handy. The family should have decided on a name prior to the Naming Ceremony.

Leader: "Before we bestow the name we have chosen on our beloved pet, I ask [*scribe's name*] to read the qualities of life that we intend for our pet as I pass the water bowl around. Once again, imagine that these happy qualities are poured into the water."

This is done.

Leader: "Who will speak about how we decided on the name we have chosen for our pet? [*Scribe's name*] will write this story in the pet journal."

A family member or members speak about the process of deciding on a name and what the name means to the family.

The leader dips his hand into the water, holding the pet tenderly, and places a few drops on the pet.

Leader: "We name you [*name of pet*], and my wish for you is...."

Everyone repeats this declaration, completing it by making a wish for the pet's life. Each person speaks directly to the pet, looking into its face and knowing that it understands.

Conclude the ceremony with treats for everyone.

. *Preparation for Moving* .

A move to a new home or business can be overwhelming. This ritual is intentionally simple so as not to add more stress to the move, yet is comforting because it assures that nothing of value will be left behind. It can be used prior to the House Blessing ritual. If an entire family is moving, each person can do this simple ritual for themselves. A single person moving can perform it for him or herself.

Materials:

    A candle, about one inch in diameter and ten to twelve inches long

    A piece of flexible parchment or decorative paper

    Ribbon or elastic band

As you pack for your move to a new location, you will make decisions about what to keep and what to leave behind. You may feel sad about something that must be discarded. When you experience gratitude, sadness, or any another emotion as you make the move to your new home, light the candle and write on the piece of parchment the quality of life you wish to take with you or the quality you wish to re-create in your new environment. For example, if a particular part of your garden is meaningful to you, you might write on the paper that a new garden will be created at your new home, or that you will create a sanctuary of peace in your new environment.

When you light the candle, imagine that the quality you desire is being drawn into the candle by the flame, just as the flame consumes oxygen from the air around it. Then blow the candle out and wrap the paper around the candle, tying it with the ribbon or elastic band. As you sort, discard, and pack, continue to write down the qualities that are important to have in your new home and burn the candle while imagining the qualities filling the flame. As you continue to prepare for your move, the scroll records the "contents" of the candle.

When you are established in your new place, choose a quiet time to untie the list from the candle. Light the candle in your new home, and read the list. As you do so, imagine that the light of the candle disperses the precious qualities into the environment of your new life, filling the space with all that was important to you from the home you left behind and spreading new qualities as well. You can reuse this candle if you do the House Blessing ritual in your new space.

. *House Blessing* .

This ritual is for a family or individual moving into a new home, but it can also be used to bless a home already inhabited. Add further blessings by inviting friends and family to participate. This ritual is written with a leader, though a single person may perform the ritual by reading the leader's words.

Materials:

    One candle for each resident of the home

    One candle in each room

    Large bowl of water with ladle

    Flower petals

    A cup or small container for each person

    Dried sage in a dish or flat shell, or rattles to shake

    Matches

Set up:

    Place the bowl of water and the petals outside the door.

    Place cups and sage near the punch bowl.

    Place a candle in each room of the house.

*I*nvite all participants to gather at the front door of the house with the large bowl filled with water nearby. The people who will live in the house hold the candles.

✢

Leader: "We are gathered here to bless the home where [*name(s) of home's inhabitants*] will live, love, rejuvenate their bodies and souls, make memories, learn lessons, welcome friends, heal hearts, and build dreams. The wishes and prayers that we offer them today are as important as the physical foundation on which the house is built, because our wishes are part of the spiritual and emotional foundation of their home. Let each of us take some petals, and, as we sprinkle them on the water, let us speak our wishes for this family."

Everyone takes a handful of petals, sprinkles them on the water in the bowl, and speaks their wishes for the family and the home.

Leader: "This water has been made holy by our wishes. We first bless the threshold of this home with the holy water. The front threshold is the boundary between your personal world and the larger world. You allow life-affirming people and energy through this doorway into your home and wisely keep life-draining energy and people outside. By blessing the threshold you claim the space inside your home to be nurturing, loving, restoring, healing, and holy for your family and those whom you invite to share your home. Take some water now and bless the doorway into your sanctuary."

The home's residents sprinkle water from the bowl on the front doorway.

Leader: "Good. Now, may we enter your home?"

Participants are invited in by residents.

Leader: "We will now light the sage and the candles held by [*name(s) of home's inhabitants*]. Sage smoke is cleansing and purifying; it cleanses old energy, energy that is not in harmony with this family. *(If anyone is sensitive to sage smoke, rattles can be shaken instead. Sound is as effective as smoke in breaking up old energy and allowing it to move away.)* The candles held by the family represent their life force that fills this home as they move from room to room. We let old energy be released and fill this home with the energy of its new family."

The sage and the candles are lit. The leader, family, and group of supportive friends move from room to room. The leader wafts the smoke into all the corners and then asks the family what they want to experience in each room, one at a time. Each family member states their wishes for themselves in each room and then lights the candle in that room.

Leader: "As we light the candle in this room, we claim the blessings that this family has called forth. This room becomes alive with the qualities that have been summoned. The home is happy to be used so well. Blessed be."

Each room of the entire house is brought to life in this way.

The group ends at the front door.

Leader: "We have called forth love in the rooms of this home in all the forms that this family has named. We have brought to life the generative energy in each space. We now seal the home in blessing by each of us taking a cup of this holy water and sprinkling it around the outside of the house with our own prayers."

Everyone takes a cup of the water from the bowl and walks around the house, sealing the outside in blessing.

Leader: "Our work here is complete. May you, [*name(s) of home's inhabitants*], live happily in this home, and may it be a sanctuary for you and your friends."

. *Job Transition Ritual* .

Changing jobs can be one of the most exciting and stressful events in life. Whether you have left a job voluntarily or not, this change can provoke fear, anger, and sadness, or inspire relief, happy anticipation, and joy —or all of these feelings and more. This ritual is designed to help a person in the process of job transition to focus on his strengths and a positive vision for his life.

The transition a person changing jobs goes through is truly a hero's journey. To understand the stages of this trek, see the Wheel of the Hero's Journey in Part Four. Leaving a job entails both the winds of change and the river of no return phases. Preparing for the next job involves the struggle and trials phase. As a hero's journey often features the helper, this ritual utilizes a "guide" in this role. The guide needs no special training; he or she should be a loving family member or friend who has the best interests of the person who is between jobs in their heart. The guide and the job seeker together will aide the seeker's transition into the place of greater skill, power, and blessing.

If you would prefer to do this ritual alone, you may assume the role of the guide through your own internalized thought process.

Materials:

The Job Change Wheel and Wheel of the Hero's Journey (found in Part Four)

Paper and writing instrument
Burning bowl
Matches
Candle

*T*he person between jobs (referred to as the "seeker" throughout this ritual) and the guide come together and create a sacred space by lighting a candle and each speaking their intentions for their work together. Both of them read the section in this book about the hero's journey starting on page 119, as well as this Job Change Ritual. The guide states his understanding of the helper's role and his commitment to it. The seeker speaks of his openness to the assistance of the guide and his willingness to do the work of the hero.

The guide readies himself for taking notes, as described below, and then offers a copy of the Wheel of the Hero's Journey to the seeker. The guide invites the seeker to share his experiences of leaving his former job and how it corresponds to the positions on the Wheel. The guide might encourage the seeker to recall experiences in detail with such questions as, "When was the first time you felt the gentle breezes of the winds of change?" or "How did you know that you were afloat on the river of no return?" or simply, "Can you tell me more?" As the seeker describes his experiences along the journey, the guide notes when he hears attitudes of fear, victimhood, self-doubt, anger, or other life-diminishing thoughts that might be released later in the ritual. He also takes notes of thoughts and feelings of positive self-assessment, and awareness of lessons learned, skills acquired, and gifts received. Care should be taken to record the thoughts of the seeker with no judgment or leading by the guide.

The guide then asks the seeker the following questions, carefully noting the answers and asking follow up questions if deeper understanding is needed.

What did you contribute, professionally and personally, in your former job?

What did you create, repair, encourage, transform, plan, supply, disassemble, or help?

How were you valued?

In your former job, what was painful and what did you wish for instead?

Were you undervalued or not well used in your former job? How?

What skills or gifts did you give in your former job that now feel finished and complete?

What do you have to give that is still in you to be given?

What are your fears as you approach your next job and what feelings would you like to feel instead?

Is there something that needs to be healed or restored in you as you move into your new work? What would that healing look and feel like?

What new ideas do you have that you would like to express?

In your ideal work situation, what is the balance of teamwork and solitary work that you want?

What are you passionate about that you would like to experience and express in your new work?

What else do you want to experience in your new work?

After the questions are asked and the responses recorded, the guide organizes the notes into three lists. The first is a list of beliefs, memories, feelings, and ways of being that the seeker is ready to release, such as various fears, grievances, anger, and the like. The second list is of work accomplishments and projects that are truly finished in the life of the seeker.

The third list of notes is organized and recorded onto the Job Change Wheel in a way that is consistent with the energies of the directions. This Wheel will form the basis of the creative process to bring the seeker and his new work together. In the eastern quadrant of the Wheel, the guide records new ideas, new goals, new explorations that the seeker revealed that he wants to experience. In the southern quadrant, the guide records the skills, support, forms of expression, and gifts to be given that the seeker envisions for himself in his new job. In the western quadrant the guide records the feelings that the seeker desires to experience in his new work. In the top of the wheel, the guide describes the most healthy and whole state of being that the seeker can envision for himself.

The guide and the seeker work together on these three lists. They discuss, edit, and reposition ideas until every empowering and disempowering thought finds its place on the documents. When they have incorporated all the responses of the seeker, they ask a final question about each list. For the first list of things to be released, they ask, "Are there any additional life-draining beliefs to be released?" For the second list they ask, "Are there any additional projects that are ready to be released?" Looking at the Job Change Wheel they ask, "Are there more important empowering ideas to be claimed?" They add anything that is revealed.

The guide makes available the bowl and matches. Taking the list of disempowering fears and other life-draining attitudes, he begins.

Guide: "The celebration of releasing and accepting is at hand.

"Are you ready to release all ways of being that are on this list? When we burn this list, the written words will be gone just as the corresponding ways of living and thinking will be gone from your heart and mind. Are you ready?"

The seeker responds affirmatively, and the guide invites him to set fire to the list. As the seeker does this, they both contemplate the flames and the releasing. The guide praises the good work done by the seeker and offers him next the list of completed goals and accomplishments.

Guide: "This is the list of what you have done in your previous work that is truly completed. Some of these accomplishments may hold great pride and joy for you, while others may just remind you that you are relieved they are over. As you burn this list, you symbolically release the creative energy that is caught in these completed projects. You are making room in yourself for more creativity. Are you ready to open to new possibilities by releasing the old?"

The seeker responds affirmatively and sets the list of previous accomplishments ablaze in the burning bowl. Once again the guide and the seeker watch the flames and affirm the good and powerful work that is being done. The guide then offers the completed Job Changing Wheel to the seeker.

Guide: "This wheel contains the new ideas, ways of expressing support, feelings, and the state of being that you desire as you open to your new work. The words written on this wheel came from the depths of your soul. They are your words. Please read all these powerful attributes and qualities aloud preceded by the words, 'I accept.'"

The seeker does this.

Guide: "You have spoken your intention into the universe. There is nothing on this Wheel that the universe does not long to give you. Therefore, all of this will come to you in the perfect ways and in the perfect time. As the universe reorganizes itself around you, I ask you to repeat this part of the ritual daily, speaking aloud those things the universe is preparing for you. This is the work that will make you the hero, ready to accept the new job or position when it is presented. You will recognize it as a gift, accompanying your transformed state, and you will return back to your new beginning—a new job, a new way of being, with new faith, skills, and enthusiasm for the work ahead. Congratulations, and blessings to you."

. *Wedding Ceremony or Sacred Union* .

Weddings are probably the most familiar of all rituals. Many people have specific ideas about what a wedding should contain and what the experience should feel like. One's spiritual tradition often dictates how the marriage ritual is performed. In truth, two people who want to spend their lives together in a marriage or in a committed relationship have complete freedom to plan their special day exactly the way they want it.

Very little is required for a wedding to be legal. The union must be recorded in a marriage license, a contract that legalizes the union in the eyes of the state and the country. Upon the receipt of a completed license, the county records the names of the couple, the place, date, officiant, and witnesses, all of which are written on the license, after which the couple is legally married. The type of wedding ceremony—what is spoken, what spiritual beliefs are expressed, what promises are made, and what steps are included—is entirely up to the couple and their desires for their special day.

The laws about who can legally officiate a wedding vary from state to state and county to county. In some counties a person with no legal or religious affiliation can become a "clerk of the court" for a day if he so applies; with that temporary title, he can perform the wedding ceremony and sign the license. In other instances a friend of the couple can perform most or all of the ceremony while a "stand in" clergy person signs the document. For situations in which a couple wishes to have a spiritual ceremony of union without a license, the officiant could be anyone they choose.

The wedding ceremony is one of the most powerful rites of passage in our culture. Although a marriage is a legally sanctioned institution in this country, most couples who marry do so because of a deep feeling of love and commitment and not because they want to comply with any law. Therefore, in a successful wedding ceremony, the couple should feel dynamically changed as they promise their love and trust to each other for their future. The skill of the officiant to create sacred space, a unified feeling for all those present, and a spiritual boundary for the couple to cross in a conscious and sacred way, makes the difference between a meaningless performance and a profound life-changing experience for all those present.

The following ceremony is just one of an infinite variety of ceremonies that is possible. It is divided into traditional sections, such as the welcome, the prayer, the charge, and the vows. If the couple wants to include a song, reading, or another special section, this can easily be inserted between the scripted parts. Following the basic wedding ceremony are several pieces which can be added into the traditional format.

Materials:

Marriage license (to be completed and mailed by officiant)
Two rings

Set up:

Rehearsal, as needed, for the procession, the ceremony logistics, and the recession.

*A*fter the guests have been seated and the wedding party is in place, the officiant begins.

✦

Welcome

Officiant: "Welcome everyone. We are gathered here today to celebrate and share in the happiness of [*groom's name*] and [*bride's name*]. Family and friends are the most important people in the world to [*groom's name*] and [*bride's name*]. You have been invited here to be a part of the coming together of these two separate lives, these two people filled with love for each other. We acknowledge and honor the love that you have given them over the years. I know your presence here blesses the beginning of their marriage. For this is their wedding day—the miraculous day when two separate lives join together in a union older than recorded history, carrying with it the reverence of countless generations and cultures the world over. People in all places at all times have witnessed in awe what you will witness here today: two people who become one union, transformed by their love and intention.

"Actually, your role is more than merely being witnesses. You represent all the people in the world who will know [*groom's name*] and [*bride's name*] as a married couple. The hopes, desires, beliefs, and vision that you bring to this experience today will help form the foundation of their married life together. So, as participants to this wonderful celebration of transformation and union, [groom's name] and [bride's name] ask that you continue to give them your love and your support and that you affirm their ever-growing love for each other in your own hearts."

Prayer

Officiant: "I believe that an occasion like this should be grounded in the sacred awareness that prayer evokes. Knowing that many spiritual faiths are represented here, I ask each of you to pray according to your own faith for [groom's name] and [bride's name]. I will also pray.

"As each of us now turns within, we acknowledge that a sacred presence descends upon all of us now, enfolding us and holding us. This sacred presence creates this into a holy place, a place between the worlds of spirit and form. It creates our work here to be of the utmost holiness. The activity of this sacred presence that we may call God is alive and vibrant here because today we are aware of the love of God in a very special way. We know that the love of God enlivens each of us here, particularly [groom's name] and [bride's name], both beloved of God and beloved to each other. We prepare ourselves to witness the love of God being created into a new form, a union of two souls coming together for the highest good and the greatest joy for each other and themselves. This union we traditionally call a marriage. We bless this marriage that is to be created here today; we bless the two loving beings who are to be transformed from a bride and a groom into a wife and a husband, and we bless each and every loving supporter present who acknowledges this union. We give thanks and accept this as the truth. Amen."

Presentation
(For a ceremony in which the bride is "given away")
Officiant: "Who has the privilege of presenting this young woman, [*bride's name*], to be married to this young man, [*groom's name*]?"

The father of the bride: "Her mother and I do."

Alternatively
Officiant: "There is an old tradition that the elders, or the wise ones of the tribe or family, give the beloveds to one another as an acknowledgment of their support for this union. I believe all of you here qualify as the tribe of [*bride's name*] and [*groom's name*]. So please all answer when I ask, 'Who has the privilege of presenting this woman, [*bride's name*], to this man, [*groom's name*]?"

All: "We do!"

Officiant: "And who has the privilege of presenting this man to this woman?"

All: "We do!"

Charge

Officiant: "[*Bride's name*] and [*groom's name*], there are no ties on earth so sweet as those to which you now commit yourselves. This union is to be undertaken with great consideration and respect for both your partner and yourself. There is no human relationship on earth more holy than the one you are about to enter. This is one of the most important decisions you will ever make. Out of all the world you have chosen each other to be your life partner. Whether you realize it or not at this moment, you will change most remarkably because of this decision.

"To be willing to enter into this marriage, you make yourselves available to a process of transformation. By the little and big joys and the little and big annoyances that you cause each other, you will each be like sandpaper on the edges that bump into each other. In fact, by choosing this particular person to love and make your life with, you have chosen to make an intimate, safe world in which you both can smooth out all the rough edges of your selves and heal any bruises on your souls. You have been unconsciously drawn to exactly the person who has those skills, attributes, frustrating traits, and blessed qualities that you need to be affected by in order to change into the person that you want and need to become. So as you promise your lives to each other today, you enter a path of no return, because personal evolution is always for expansion and further expression.

"Simply put, life will never be the same for you. For no matter how long and how well you have known each other, there will be a deepening that is profound, especially if you welcome it. I encourage you to give yourselves with abandon to this marriage. Love deeply; don't hold back, and believe that in sharing your two lives in complete trust, openness, passion, compassion, and courage, surprising blessings will pour into the container that is your marriage. Your marriage will change through the years as you both change, but the unchanging commitment of your mutual love will allow both of you to share life's magnificence in ways that you have not known before.

"Before you make your promises to each other, take a moment as single people for the last time to look out at your family and friends who love you and who support your togetherness. I would like to speak of some of the things that all of us wish for you.

"First, we wish a love for you that makes both of you happy people, that continues to give you a joy and a zest for living through the years.

"We wish for you that the vision you have of one another at this moment will never be dimmed. We wish that your vision of each other will deepen and grow in respect and love. We wish that this vision will expand in peace and harmony so that your home is blessed and your larger circle of friends and acquaintances is blessed. May it be that the power of your loving marriage expands and contributes to greater peace for the whole world.

"Finally, we wish that throughout your life together you will individually be able to love yourselves more deeply because you are treasured by your mate, and that you come to see the light in everyone more easily because you can see the light so clearly in your beloved."

Vows

Officiant: "[*Bride's name*] and [*groom's name*], today your separate lives with their individual memories, dreams, and desires merge into one. Today you enter a new life together that will draw both of you up to new levels of joy, sensitivity, and challenge. This is the moment in which you offer the fullness of your hearts to bless one another. You have found each other, and the whole world is blessed by your union. Are you ready to make your marriage promises to each other?"

Both: "I am."

Officiant: "Will you [*bride's name*] and you [*groom's name*] bring the very best that you are into this marriage for your own sake and for the sake of the other?"

Both: "I will."

Officiant: "Will you please join hands and face each other?"

The couple does so.

Officiant (to groom): "[*Groom's name*], do you take [*bride's name*], whose hands you hold, choosing her alone to be your wedded wife? Do you promise to live with her, talk with her, love her, comfort her, work with her, play with her, honor her at all times and be faithful to her?"

Groom: "I do."

Officiant (to bride): "[*Bride's name*], do you take [*groom's name*], whose hands you hold, choosing him alone to be your wedded husband? Do you promise to live with him, talk with him, love him, comfort him, work with him, play with him, honor him at all times and be faithful to him?"

Bride: "I do."

Officiant: "[*Groom's name*], please repeat after me: [*Bride's name*], I take you as my beloved wife and dearest friend. I promise to share my life openly with you, and to speak the truth to you in love. I promise to honor you and tenderly care for you. From this day forward, I promise to cherish you and to encourage your own fulfillment and peace through all the changes of our lives."

Officiant (to groom): "What gift do you give to [*bride's name*] as a symbol of your love and commitment?"

Groom: "A ring."

The groom hands the ring to the minister. The bride and groom each put a finger on the ring as it lies in the minister's palm.

Officiant: "This ring, without beginning or ending, has long been recognized as the symbol of eternity. This ring therefore stands for the eternality of your love for each other. Bless this ring, O God. Bless [*groom's name*] who gives it and [*bride's name*] who will wear it."

Officiant: "[*Groom's name*], please repeat after me: I give this ring from my heart to your hand. With it I pledge to you the treasures of my mind, my body, and my soul. I give you my trust, my tomorrows, and ask you to accept me as your husband."

Officiant: "[*Bride's name*], please repeat after me: [*groom's name*], I take you as my beloved husband and dearest friend. I promise to share my life openly with you, and to speak the truth to you in love. I promise to honor you and tenderly care for you. From this day forward, I promise to cherish you and to encourage your own fulfillment and peace through all the changes of our lives."

Officiant (to bride): "What gift do you give to [*groom's name*] as a symbol of your love and commitment?"

Bride: "A ring."

Once again, the ring is handed to the minister. The bride and groom each put a finger on the ring as it lies in the minister's palm.

Officiant: "This ring also stands for the never-ending love between the two of you. Bless this ring, O God. Bless [*bride's name*] who gives it and [*groom's name*] who will wear it."

Officiant: "[*Bride's name*], please repeat after me: I give this ring from my heart to your hand. With it I pledge to you the treasures of my mind, my body, and my soul. I give you my trust, my tomorrows, and ask you to accept me as your wife."

Pronouncement

Officiant: "In as much as you, [*bride's name*] and you, [*groom's name*] have consented together to this union of marriage, and have declared your sacred promises to each other in the presence of God and all these wonderful family and friends, and have pledged your constancy and love for each other, I now pronounce you husband and wife. You may kiss each other."

This concludes the wedding ceremony. Following are several pieces that can be added according to the wishes of the couple.

Parent Vows

Young people often want this formal parental acceptance for the mate they have chosen. It fits into the basic ceremony after the prayer and in place of the other examples of the "Presentation."

The officiant first asks the parents of the bride to stand and face the groom.

Officiant [to the bride's parents]: "[*Parents' names*], as [*groom's name*] marries your daughter, do you accept him into your family with love and respect?"

Both: "We do."

Officiant: "Will you honor the marriage he has with your daughter?"

Both: "We will."

Officiant: "Will you love him as if he were your own son?"

Both: "We will."

Officiant: "So now, [*parents' names*], do you give [*bride's name*] to be married to [*groom's name*]?"

Both: "We do."

The process is reversed with the parents of the groom.

Young Children's Vows

If the bride and/or the groom have children from a previous marriage, it is meaningful to have formal promises of love and support between the future stepparent and the children. The following words would be appropriate for young children included in the ceremony. This part of the ritual could go after the charge and before the vows. The example shown is for promises between the children of the groom from a previous marriage and the bride, who will become the new stepmother.

The officiant calls the groom's children forward to stand facing the bride.

Officiant: "With the marriage of [*bride's name*] and [*groom's name*], you all become a new family. Although [*bride's name*] will never take the place of your mom, she will be a very important person in your lives. Families work and play together. They love one another, and they respect one another. Are you ready to take the vows to create this new family?"

Children and bride respond affirmatively.

Officiant: "As [*bride's name*] marries your dad, you have a new stepmom and a new family to interact with. Do you promise to love this new family and to live and learn as best you can in this family? Do you promise to respect each family member and hold your best wishes for each one in your hearts?"

Children: "We do."

Officiant: "[*Bride's name*], as you marry [*groom's name*], you take on the joyful and challenging role of being a stepmother to [*names of groom's children*]. Do you promise to be as good an example, as wise an advisor, and as loving a parent as you can be for these children, and do you promise to love them as your own?"

Bride: "I do."

Officiant: "You have all promised to love and honor one another. So, as your parents are pronounced husband and wife, you all become the new, united, committed [*family's new last name*] family. Right now, you children may be seated again."

Older Children's Vows

In the case of a couple with older children, teenage or beyond, who are essentially grown, the immediate influence of a stepparent will not be felt. However, it is meaningful to include these older children in the new family configuration, if everyone wishes it. This example is for older children of the bride making loving promises with the groom.

The minister or officiant calls the bride's children forward to stand facing the groom.

Officiant: "With the marriage of [*bride's name*] and [*groom's name*], you all become a
new family. Although [*groom's name*] will not be the man to raise you, he will
be a very important person in your lives. You all will be very important in
each others' lives. Harmony and mutual support create a family feeling
among all of you. Are you ready to take the vows to create this new, extended family?"

All respond affirmatively.

Officiant: "[*Childrens' names*], do you accept [*groom's name*] as your mother's husband?
Do you promise to do what you can to promote family love and harmony?
Do you promise to speak the truth in love to everyone in this family and to
hold your best wishes for each family member in your hearts?"

Children: "We do."

Officiant: "[*Groom's name*], do you accept [*childrens' names*] as your wife's children, thereby making them very important loved ones in your new family? Do you promise to nurture them, counsel with them, and hold them in respect and love?"

Groom: "I do."

Officiant: "You have all promised to love and honor one another. So, as [*bride's name*] and [*groom's name*] are pronounced husband and wife, you all become the new, united, committed [*family's last name*] family. Right now, you may be seated again."

Rose Ceremony
This imbedded ceremony is to honor the family love that has been given in the lives of the bride and groom before the moment they marry and create their own family unit. It is usually done with the mothers of the bride and groom. It can, however, be performed with any special family members or friends who signify lifelong love for the two being married. The two people chosen for the Rose Ceremony each carry a long-stemmed rose from the processional throughout the ceremony until the time for the Rose Ceremony, which fits nicely after the vows and before the pronouncement.

Officiant: "Before the official pronouncement which announces [*bride's name*] and [*groom's name*] as a married couple, we want to perform the Rose Ceremony, which honors the love that these two have received for their whole lives, that love that nurtured them into the fine adults before you today, ready and willing to commit their love to each other for their lifetime. The mothers of [*bride's name*] and [*groom's name*] are each carrying a rose; this rose represents the lifelong love that has surrounded these two. I would like to invite the moms forward to give their rose to their child with their blessing."

The moms come forward, hand the roses to their children, and give them hugs in blessing; then they sit down again.

Officiant (to couple): "The rose has long been considered the symbol of love. You have just been given your first gift as a formally committed couple, the gift of love. Now, I would like you to exchange roses, please."

The couple does so.

Officiant: "You have just given each other your first gift as a committed couple; appropriately, it is the gift of love.

"Now, I would like you to look closely at your rose. It is beautiful, strong, sturdy, a perfect gift to whomever looks upon it, just as each of you is strong, beautiful, a gift to all of us and especially to each other. However, I would like you to look even closer at your rose and see if you can spot an imperfection, a bent leaf or a discolored petal. Notice that these flaws do not mar the perfection of the rose. This is like the two of you as well. Have you noticed if your partner has any flaws? Part of the magic of marriage is to notice the flaws and have it be easier and easier to include the flaws in the perfection of your love and acceptance of each other.

"Now, I would like you to both put your hands around both roses like a vase. Notice how the roses are even more beautiful because they are together. They are a matched pair, each bringing out the loveliness of the other. This is like the two of you, also. Each of you is more radiant, more beautiful, more available to life because you are together. However, like the roses that still bear their flaws even though they are together, you two, also, will still have those flaws that may even seem more pronounced because you are married. May it be that the love in your marriage grows to include every detail of your mate's personality and traits, and grows more beautiful through the years because you are together.

"I would like you to have a place for roses in your home. On the anniversary of this occasion, each year, if each of you would bring a rose to that special place, it will speak of the commitment you made here today and reaffirm your love and devotion to each other. Also, in any marriage there come those times when the flaws are easier to see than the perfection. At those times as well, if one or both of you would bring a rose to that special place, it will speak of the love that is the basis of your life together. It will help you get through times of challenge and back to the feeling that lives in you both today.

"Now, in order to complete the circle of love, I would like you to give your rose back to your new mother-in-law."

The couple does so and returns to the officiant for the pronouncement and the kiss.

. *Ritual for Divorce or Ending a Relationship* .

The end of a relationship is a passage that can be very painful, but ritual can help alleviate the hurt and hasten the healing. This ritual helps a couple reach closure with their marriage or relationship in a way that the legal paperwork of divorce can never accomplish, allowing each partner to gracefully end an important chapter in his or her life and wish the other well. This ritual works best after the couple has been physically separated for a time, allowing each person time to gain some perspective and calm the raw emotions of breaking up.

I've written this ritual as officiated by a third party, but it can also be performed by only the two people involved. One person can even perform this separating ritual by him or herself. Wishes for the well-being of a former partner and releasing them to their own life path can be done successfully even if the partner is not present. If you are alone and performing this ritual, use the officiant's words as your own intentions. You might rewrite the script and use "I" in place of "you" or "we." Read the vows out loud, as declarations to your own heart and mind.

Materials:

Any symbol of the marriage, such as the rings

☥

Officiant: "We are gathered to conclude an important chapter in both your lives. Conscious closure allows you to see the gifts that have come to you in this marriage, which is coming to an end; it allows you to have a new beginning, free of the old. Today your marriage, which joined your lives and souls together, comes to an end. It is a time to feel the finality of completion.

"First, to honor the gifts that were given in this marriage, I would like each of you to tell what gifts you received from the other when you were together as a married couple."

They both briefly share the gifts they received.

Officiant: "Please now repeat after me *(leading first one and then the other to repeat)*: 'Thank you for the gifts you gave me in our marriage. I am changed for the better because of you.'

"Sometimes a union that was perfect in its time completes its purpose and is no longer right or appropriate. So it seems to be with the two of you. You were called together, and now you are called apart. This is not because of a defect in either of you. This conclusion should be undertaken with great consideration and respect for your former partner as well as yourself, for ending a marriage is a deep matter for your two lives and your two souls. You have considered this decision greatly; is that correct?"

Couple: "We have."

Officiant: "Do each of you feel that all that could be done to make this a happy marriage for the two of you was done, and that the wise and compassionate course of action to take now is to end your marriage?"

Couple: "We do."

Officiant: "We need to retrace the steps in commitment you made on your wedding day so you can free each other of the promises you made and free yourselves to walk a different path. Do you [*name*] and you [*name*] wish to free each other of promises, commitments, and agreements that brought you together as a married couple?"

Couple: "We do."

Officiant: "Please now repeat after me *(leading first one and then the other to repeat)*: '[*Name*], I free you from the vows you made to me on our wedding day. From this day forward, love, faithfulness, sharing of resources, and emotional support are not mine to expect from you. Your future is your own. I honor you for all you have been in my life, and I release both of us from the marriage we had.'"

Couple: "Do you have symbols of the marriage?"

The couple produce the rings and give them to the officiant.

Officiant: "These rings which were the symbol of your committed love together are transformed back into simple jewelry. They are no longer symbols of a marriage."

The officiant speaks of the couple's plan for the rings and returns them to the appropriate people.

Officiant: "Even though your marriage is over, may you treat each other with kindness should you interact in the future. When you think of each other in times to come, may it be with gratitude and compassion. Is this also your wish?"

Couple: "It is."

Officiant: "Good. Then each of you, please repeat after me: 'Our paths, which were together, now separate. Thank you for all you are and all you gave. I bless you on your way. May life be good to you, and may you find great happiness.'
   "I honor both of you for creating more peace through this ending rather than more conflict. May your lives from this moment forward be filled

with light, and may you be blessed in deep and surprising ways as you move forward in your individual lives. And so, because it is your mutual wish to end this marriage, I declare each of you, [name] and [name], to be free, single, and on your own. Go now your separate ways, and know that, with God, you are never alone."

If the friends of the couple are attending the ritual, the two newly single people turn apart and walk to their friends, who receive them with love. If no others are present, the couple may shake hands or embrace and leave the room peacefully.

Ritual of a Woman's Wisdom Time

The Ritual of a Woman's Wisdom Time honors women who have reached menopause. "The change of life," as it is called, is often not a transition of magic and empowerment for women today. Rather, it can be filled with many kinds of distress, from disturbing physical symptoms to the fear that comes with aging and the loss of youth. This ceremony helps restore the blessing of the passage into a woman's wisdom time. It will benefit all the women who participate because it reveals positive, empowering truths: that each age has its richness, that there are gifts to be given and received at every stage of life, and that there is really nothing to fear about our physical transitions on earth.

This ritual is for a group of adult females, but it could also include young girls of the family of the woman being honored. The ritual can be adapted to honor several women who are celebrating their menopause. You may even use this ritual as a guide for honoring yourself, alone, as you enter the wisdom time in your life. If you perform this ritual alone, use the leader's words as a self blessing. Instead of speaking the answers to the questions that are asked in the ritual, write them in your journal. When you walk through the portal that you create for yourself, ask for blessings from the goddess energy that is all around you. Create a symbol for yourself of this transition that you infuse with the wisdom and power that is now yours.

Materials:

    Candles, enough to create a circle around the group of women

    A decorated portal, which could be an arch or simply two chairs with their backs facing each other to form an opening

    An altar, on which is the following:

        Food (as described in the ritual)

        Personal symbols of the woman being honored

        A potted plant

        A small pitcher of milk

        A decorated chair

        A celebration garment

        Drums

        A spinning wheel, if available

Set up:

    Set the candles in a circle around the room.

    Erect the portal in the center of the circle, so that the seating area can be divided into two semi-circles around it.

    Place candles along the diameter of the circle to emphasize the semi-circles. Within one semi-circle, place the altar, the spinning wheel, and enough seating for all the women; in the other, set up the drums and the decorated chair with the celebration garment laid across it.

Prior to the ritual:

The woman being honored should bring food or fragrances that remind her of three eras of her life: her childhood, her maidenhood, and her life as a wife, mother, partner, or single adult. One tiny morsel of food for each participant is sufficient. For example, if peanut butter and jelly sandwiches are the symbol of her childhood, individual bite-sized pieces of sandwich are fine.

The participants of the ceremony should make the honoree a garment that is easy to slip on, like a caftan.

*T*he group of women gathers in the semi-circle with the leader and the person being honored sitting on each side of the altar. The leader, a woman past her menopause, begins.

☩

Leader: "We are gathered here for the Ritual of a Woman's Wisdom Time, known in ancient times as the Rite of the Fourteenth Moon. Today we bear witness to the mystery of life and its physical transition in us as women, and particularly in our beloved [*name of honoree*]. In order to sanctify our proceedings and to honor this space, I ask you to create a sacred circle, actually a sacred semi-circle. Please light the candles that outline the half of the circle in which we sit one at a time. As you light a candle, please call out the names of your mothers and grandmothers so that the wisdom and energy of our ancestors can be with us."

The women do this, and the leader continues.

Leader: "The Ritual of a Woman's Wisdom Time is performed when one of us has thoroughly passed through the change of life signified by the ceasing of our monthly blood flow. The beginning of our flow was a gift from the goddess when we entered our time of maidenhood. Each month for forty years or so, we stood in the possibility that a soul could come through us to be born into the world. Many of us have experienced that blessing. Just as the door is opened by the goddess, it is closed by the goddess in our midlife. So it is with [*name*]. Today we honor the mystery of the closing of one doorway in our beloved [*name*].

"It has been at least a year and a day between her last blood flow and now. This ritual reminds us that in ancient times our bodies were perfectly aligned with the phases of the moon. Our blood flowed when the moon was full. Thirteen full moons happen in a year, and thirteen times our blood flowed in a year. So the marking of the fourteenth moon since our last flow was the ancient timetable for the completion cycle of a year and a day. The Ceremony of the Fourteenth Moon indicated that a woman had finished the transition between her fertile time and the beginning of her wisdom time. It is both the transition and the woman who has made this transition, [*name*], that we honor today.

"Dear [*name*], speak to us of the ending of your cycles, so that your sisters may share this time with you and our daughters may hear of this transition without the cultural myths and thoughtless humor."

The woman being honored tells of her time of menopause. This can be very healing since women do not usually focus on this transition of life in a conscious, compassionate way. The woman might share fears of aging, descriptions of physical discomfort, relief that her bleeding time is over, and/or changes in her sexual interests.

Leader: "There are physical changes during this time of life that have been misunderstood by our modern culture. We know that in this life there are cycles. We see cycles in the seasons, in the day and night hours, and in the eras of our life. It is not always spring, and we are not always youthful, but just as there are blessings of autumn and winter, so there are blessings in the era of our life after our fertile time. It is in the places where modern culture fears this change where we look for the blessings. For example, during menopause we move into a time of life in which we have a vision of the whole world. Our physical sight changes, and it is easier for us to see into the far distance. We move into a life era in which we serve the world with our creativity and wisdom instead of serving the life that we birth. With this change we become rewired for service to the larger world, so our nervous system reorients itself with new energy as the life force rises within us. After midlife we have greater vision, more creativity, and powerful energy to accomplish work for all of humanity, if we choose to let our physical changes serve our purpose in life. May this be so for you, dear [name].

"In our culture there is fear about a woman growing into a crone, a word that holds much power but is resisted in modern culture. We are here to help heal that fear in ourselves and in those we love, so that the positive power of cronehood can flourish in our beloved [name] and in our world. The fear of cronehood is about growing unattractive and physically unable to do the things that a younger person can do. Our human tendency is to demonize what we fear. So the crone, once revered for her wisdom and life experience, has in recent times (and by that I mean the last several hundred years) been turned into 'the hag' and 'the witch.'

"From the twelfth to the eighteenth centuries in Europe, and during the 1600s in America, thousands of women were tortured and killed for being witches. Often the only evidence of a woman being a witch was that she was old and repugnant to the investigators. An important reason for us to be together today is to heal the cultural fear and revulsion about a woman growing older, so that it will be easier for our daughters to celebrate their movement through midlife when it is their time. To assist with this healing we have a spinning wheel with us, a symbol of the crone in myth and fairy tale. The spinning of the wheel reminds us of the cycles of our lives. The thread that is spun is the thread of our lifetime. The crone goddesses of many cultures are the ones who cut the thread at the end of our lives. It is easier to see the blessing of the cutting of the thread and the return to the goddess when the crone time of our life is revered.

"[*Name*], before you walk through the portal of midlife into your wisdom time, into your cronehood, let us share the eras of your life with you. This is the time to appreciate your accomplishments and let go of things in your life that are over. You are invited to do this with us, your dear friends and family who love you and hold you in our highest vision.

"[*Name*], you have brought food and aromas to share with us that symbolize the previous three eras of your life. The sense of smell is the deepest, psychically. Smells can bring us right back to the first time and place we smelled them. So, please take a bite or a smell of the substance that reminds you of your childhood. Close your eyes, savor it, bring back the images of that time, and then share the food or aroma and memories with your sisters. Let us eat the substance of your life so we may know you and love you more deeply.

"Now, share your treasures with us, these physical symbols you have placed on the altar. Tell us of the joy and pain, the accomplishments and disappointments of your childhood."

The woman being honored follows these directions, and when she is finished the leader spins the spinning wheel.

Leader: "I spin the wheel as the goddess spun the early years of your life. We receive and bless this era. *(She leads the women who repeat after her.)* We celebrate your joys with you; we grieve your sadness with you. You are our beloved sister."

The group continues in this manner, sharing, witnessing, and blessing the eras of maidenhood and adulthood with the woman being honored. After each sharing time the leader spins the spinning wheel.

Leader: "I spin the wheel as the goddess spun the maiden years and then the adult years of your life. We receive and bless this era. *(She leads the women who repeat after her.)* We celebrate your joys with you; we grieve your sadness with you.

You are our beloved sister."

Leader: "It is almost time to leave these eras of your life behind you. It is important to consciously let these go before new blessings and opportunities can come to you. Beloved [name], I have here in this pitcher a small amount of milk. It symbolizes that the possibility of milk flowing from your breasts is now over, just as blood flowing from your womb and the possibility of babies being formed in your body is also over. Please take this pitcher of milk and tell us what else is finished in your life. When you are complete I invite you to pour the milk into the earth around this plant. The earth takes much of what we release and transforms it. This act signifies that you are surrendering to change and are ready for what is to emerge next in your life."

The woman being honored follows these directions.

Leader: "It is time for those of us who have already passed into our wisdom time to precede [name] into the second half of the sacred circle and prepare the way for her."

The women who have already passed menopause file through the portal. They light the candles that surround the space and invoke the crone goddesses, among whom are:

Yemaya—West African goddess and mother of all
Hecate—Greek goddess of the crossroads and life's passages
Cerridwen—Celtic goddess who boils the caldron of life and death
Baubo—Greek goddess of bawdy sexual humor
Changing Woman—Navajo goddess of transformation

Leader: "Beloved [*name*], the time has come for you to be born into the wisdom time of your life. Please step to the edge of the portal and let your sisters who have not yet reached your stage of life speak to you."

The women who are still experiencing their monthly cycles offer words of support and love to the woman being honored, who is facing them with her back to the portal.

Leader: "Dear [*name*], please face the portal. We ask you to disrobe and prepare yourself for this mystical transition as when you were born into this life."

The woman removes her clothes, and the leader continues as the women in the second semicircle begin to drum softly.

Leader: "The half of the sacred circle you are about to enter represents the second half of your life which holds many blessings for you. You have surrendered all you can from your previous life; you take with you the qualities which support life in any era—love, vision, creativity, friendships, family—and now you walk through the portal into your new life."

The drums increase in volume; the younger women hold the hands and feet of the honoree lightly so that, with a bit of pulling, she breaks free, walks through the portal, and is embraced by the leader who puts the celebration garment over her head.

Leader: "This new garment symbolizes the gifts of the second half of your life. It has been made intentionally for you for this occasion, and we will now tell you what the colors and symbols mean."

The honored woman is seated in the decorated chair and is told about her new garment.

Leader: "As in any initiation, there is a time to share information which you in your new station in life are entitled to hear. We also allow the younger women to listen so that we all may heal from any negative cultural beliefs about this time of life. I ask your sisters who have established themselves in the wisdom time of their lives to share anything they think is valuable."

The honored woman in the celebration chair and the younger women, still in the first semi-

circle, listen while the crones share their wisdom.

Leader: "One more part of this wonderful celebration remains, and it is for our honored one to complete. It is about creation in this phase of her life. You begin with a clean canvas on which to write your aspirations so that the goddess and friends who love you may support you in creating what you came to earth to accomplish. Dear [*name*], we ask you, now that you have reached this glorious time in your life, what are your dreams and how may we support you?"

The honored woman speaks her plans and desires for this time in her life.

All participants: "May it be so for you, dear [*name*]."

Leader: "We have completed our sacred work. A transformation has taken place in this space. As we close the circle, we know the work done here affects the world only for good and healing. Let us close the circle by blowing out the candles and removing the portal. Blessed be."

. *Tributes* .

*H*onoring one who has reached a milestone, gone beyond the regular demands of life, or accomplished something marvelous not only empowers the one being honored, but also satisfies those doing the honoring. Birthday celebrations, job promotions or retirement parties, get-togethers for any type of congratulation are all rituals of tribute. The reason for the gatherings differ, but the purpose is always the same: to come together to honor someone who has accomplished a great thing.

A meaningful tribute ritual always includes testimonies from the participants telling the honoree how his accomplishment has touched them personally. A gift is given to the honoree as a reminder that his or her work has served others in a powerful way. Since every tribute is specific to the occasion and the person being honored, this section does not provide scripted rituals, rather samples of some of the tributes I have created in the past. Use them as templates to be adapted for the specific tribute you wish to bestow on a group or individual.

Healing and Empowering Ritual

*W*hen a friend's young daughter was sexually touched by a boy at school, her retribution against him resulted in both students being suspended from school. Her mother and her mother's friends were worried that the wrong message had been communicated to the teenage girl. To heal and support the girl through this difficult time, several women came together and created a ritual with the teenager.

Her mother purchased several metal charms and other material to create a necklace. The charms were symbols of a sun, a hand, a unicorn, a heart, and an open book, among others. Each participating woman chose a charm that held a personal meaning for her, which she gave as a healing gift to the teenage girl during the ritual.

The women and the young teenager gathered and talked over the incident. The older women shared experiences from their lives, how they had handled them and how they had felt. The experiences ran the spectrum: some wise and empowering, some unskilled and filled with shame. Through the sharing, the teenager began to feel herself as a part of a community of women ready to support her through any situation.

Then, one at a time, each woman presented the teenager with the charm she had chosen and told its symbolic story. There were blessings bestowed of authentic power, clear communication, precious value, and deep compassion. As the charms were given, the girl's mother strung them on a cord. At the end of the evening the teenager was presented with a necklace of power to remind her of the support she had from all the women who loved her.

Group Painting

I have adapted this ritual for many circumstances, including a bridal shower, a birthday celebration, even an employee taking leave from a job. In this ritual the friends of the honoree paint pictures, symbols, or words that signify what the honored person means to them. When finished and put together, the complete painting embodies the contribution of the person being honored and becomes a work of art representing his or her service in the world.

You will need a stretched canvas on a frame, some good acrylic paints, and some brushes from an art store.

In the instance of the employee who was leaving, everyone in the office painted symbols, pictures, and words randomly over the canvas. Another employee, herself an artist, unified all the little pictures with color and lines so the finished painting was cohesive, balanced, and beautiful, as well as meaningful.

For the bridal shower and birthday, the canvas was divided into squares, one for each participant to paint in with the symbols, letters, or pictures that were meaningful to them. Each square was a work of art in itself, but when put all together, made a memorable piece that powerfully honored the person's life.

Album of Letters

I have used this ritual for birthdays, retirement, service milestones, and memorials. Purchase a scrapbook and create a greeting template that can be given to those participating. These templates should be pieces of parchment paper that will fit into the scrapbook. On each piece, write the words "You mean so much to me because...." Everyone invited to the tribute receives a copy of the template and is encouraged to complete the sentence and add photos or other special decoration. A scrapbook of all the finished letters is assembled before the tribute or during the celebration, and the book is presented to the honoree as a memento of his or her contribution.

In the case of the memorial, we gave the scrapbook to the family of the deceased person. They lived far from the deceased's group of friends, so it served as a statement to the family of all that their dear daughter and sister had meant to her smaller family group and friends where she had lived.

Bestowing a Garment of Power

*I*n many academic and spiritual traditions, a formal garment, such as a ministerial robe, a doctor's hood, or a royal crown bestows the recognition that a person has achieved a certain status in his or her field. With some imagination, capes, sashes, headdresses or any unique garment appropriate to a particular role or station could be bestowed in a ceremonial way. It deepens the experience if the presenting leader or dignitary shares the symbolism and history of the garment being bestowed with all of those present.

Before the presentation of the garment the leader encourages all of those present to bless the garment. An example of a tribute offered to a new minister receiving a stole might be: "All of you here will benefit from the transformation you witness tonight. This stole represents the new level of spiritual wisdom and clarity that your beloved minister has attained. You, here, are the ones who will continue to bless him by your presence and your open, teachable hearts. In order that he may be lifted up to his greatest capacity to give, I ask you, each and every one of you here, to call forth from the depths of yourself the greatest blessing that you can bestow on your minister. I will walk down the aisle with this stole that soon will rest on his shoulders. Please take the hand of the person sitting next to you and pass your blessing silently through your connected hands, passing and accumulating the blessings toward the aisle. Those people sitting on the aisle, would you touch this stole, pouring all the blessings into it. May it be that every time your minister puts on this stole, for years to come, he will remember your faces here tonight and your linked hands and hearts that bless his ministry, which is the ministry that serves you."

Hospice Workers' Tribute to Those Clients Who Have Passed

*F*or this tribute honoring the families and deceased loved ones that a hospice staff had served, we created a dream catcher. From the Native American tradition, dream catchers are roughly woven webs of string over a frame made from branches that can be hung above the place you sleep. It is said that a dream catcher catches the powerful and beneficial dreams while allowing the frightening dreams to pass through the spaces of the web. You can create a dream catcher for any person or group that wishes to capture beneficial ideas and release disempowering ones.

First, the hospice workers fashioned a circular frame with branches from a wisteria plant, although grapevines, ivy, or any flexible, long, slender branches are also suitable. This formed the frame for a dream catcher. Each worker then took a yard of colored ribbon and a pen.

In a meditative process, the hospice workers were asked three questions: What is your deepest wish for your clients who have passed? What is your deepest wish for their families? and What is your deepest wish for yourself as you do this loving work? The participants meditated on their answers and wrote their responses on the ribbons.

Then, one at a time, they shared with the group a particularly touching experience from their work that year as they wove their ribbon onto the branch frame. As the ribbons were added, the dream catcher took shape. The compassionate wishes of the hospice workers for the clients and families who meant so much to them communicated the love that was part of that organization. The dream catcher embodied that by catching the love while letting the sadness pass through. At the end of the tribute, the hospice had a beautiful piece of art to hang on the wall.

. *Memorial Ritual* .

The Memorial Ritual is in the same category as the Baby Blessing and Wedding Ceremony, in that it is a holy rite practiced by most religions of the world. Various denominations have their own version of these three rituals, in which they put forth their belief system. As you honor the life of a dear one who has passed on, you may include any religious content you choose in your ritual of remembrance. However, the ceremony can be sacred without a particular belief system put forth.

In this ceremony the physical remains of the deceased person are not present; it is a ceremony of remembrance only.

Special music or readings of favorite sacred scripture or poems may be included by the family unless the person being remembered has left requests for his or her own special music or written words. These readings or songs can be inserted between the activities described. This memorial ceremony is less formal that a funeral because of the amount of sharing. A rigid time limit should be avoided, if possible.

Materials:

    A large sheet of butcher paper

    Markers, stickers, and scrapbook materials

    A journal or scrapbook

Photos of the person being remembered
Notepaper with envelopes for each person
Burning bowl and matches
Food and beverages

Prior to the ritual:

All participants are invited to create a page for the scrapbook. Templates may have been previously sent out with the beginning sentence, "[*Name of person being remembered*], you changed my life for the better because...." A volunteer collects the pages and puts the scrapbook together.

Attach butcher paper to a wall on which the decades of the deceased person's life are indicated so that each ten-year period has a large space which can be filled with memories and photos. Markers and scrapbook materials are available to create this storyboard.

Create an altar with photos of the deceased, the burning bowl, and any other significant items.

*A*s people arrive, they give their completed template paper to the person assembling the scrapbook. Food should be available. Participants are asked to write on the storyboard. Include photos both in the scrapbook and on the storyboard.

The ritual may be led by a member of the clergy or someone close to the deceased, or the responsibility can be passed around to various friends and family.

φ

Leader: "Beloveds, we are gathered here today to consider with reverence, love, and respect the ongoing nature of life, and to delve into the mystery of life of one dear to us, [*name*]. We are here to remember [*name*], to share stories of his or her life, to support each other as we feel all kinds of feelings, and to remind ourselves that our time on this beautiful earth is short. It is good not to be surprised by the transition we call death, but to keep our awareness of it with us always so that we make the greatest use of our time and energy in this lifetime.

"It is at an occasion such as this that our thoughts turn to what we believe about the Eternal. If each one of you would center yourselves in a blessing or prayer according to your own faith, I will remain silent for a moment."

Everyone prays.

A brief synopsis of the person's life is spoken by the leader or by a family member. This synopsis includes the date and location of his birth, where he went to school, what work he did, who he married, names of children and grandchildren, and highlights of his life. His date of leaving his body is also spoken.

Leader: "Though these milestones are important, they don't tell the full story of this life. That is for you to do now. We have people from many different aspects of this beloved person's life. A nurturing part of a celebration such as this is to hear the stories from people who know different facets of [*name*]'s life. As you feel led, please come forward and share your deep knowing of this person. Feel free to refer to the storyboard so that a context can be built for [*name*]'s entire life."

Those present tell their stories.

Leader: "This storyboard symbolizes the dash between the two dates that commemorate the time of [*name*]'s first and last breath. It tells of [*name*]'s adventures on this earth. However, it is impossible for most of us to conceive of an ending to the energy that we knew to be [*name*]'s life. There are stories and teachings in every spiritual tradition about life beyond the realm of form, and most of us believe that immortality is a reality that we cannot fully explain but that we feel. I invite you now to stand to one side or the other of the paper that represents [*name*]'s life on earth and speak what you know to be true about the world of the immortal. We welcome stories of experiences with people who have gone on. Perhaps some of you have been contacted by [name] already. We also welcome sharing of what is unknown, unclear, hoped for, or imagined. Let the wisdom within you speak of what it knows of life everlasting."

Everyone speaks of their beliefs or experiences of immortality, and then the leader continues.

Leader: "Immortality seems to be an accepted truth to most, and yet the fact that we will not be able to touch or interact with the form of [name] again is so, so sad. It is one of the mysteries of life that the breaking or tearing open of our hearts through sadness liberates the contents of our hearts to bless the world. I ask you now to consider what is in your heart that longs to be set free. Is it a love so powerful that it is frightening? Is it a creative project that has languished because the passion to create it is stuck? I will be silent for a moment while each of you turns within and asks this question: What have I been holding in my heart that longs to be set free?"

A long moment of silence.

Leader: "I now will pass to each of you a piece of notepaper and an envelope. Please fold the paper in half, and on both halves write that which your heart longs to set free."

This is accomplished.

Leader: "I now ask you to fully experience the feelings you hold of [*name*]'s passing. Let sadness well up in you if this is what you feel. Even though grieving has its own timetable, let your feelings of loss fill your heart to overflowing right now. When you have experienced these feelings as strongly as possible, symbolize the tearing open of your heart by tearing your notepaper in half."

This is done.

Leader: "I invite you now to address the envelope to yourself, put one half of the paper in the envelope, and seal it. Bring the other half of the paper up to the altar and place it in the burning bowl, speaking aloud if appropriate that which your heart longs to set free. Then give the sealed envelope to me."

This is all accomplished.

Leader: "We now set fire to these declarations of your hearts. We send these budding ideas, dreams, and desires into the sacred place where support for their creation resides. It is true that when a person who has held an important place in our lives passes, the gift of tremendous energy is released by his passing. It is our blessing to receive this energy. You have declared what your heart longs to express, and your hearts have been torn open by the creative feelings of sadness. May it be that this gift of energy from [*name*] serves to bring forth the desired expression of your heart. One year from today I will mail these envelopes to you so that you may give thanks for the miracles in your lives which were born today."

The leader invites the family or friends who will receive the scrapbook and storyboard to sit in front of the assembled group.

Leader: "You have been the closest to our beloved [*name*], who has passed into immortality. Although [*name*] has passed from our touch and our sight, [*name*]'s life will be felt by us for the rest of our lives. We would like to share with you some of the blessings that your beloved gave the rest of us and give you these physical symbols of [*name*]'s life to keep. I ask you now to come forward one at a time and share with the family and all of us what gifts you received from [*name*]."

Various people come forward and share their experiences of what they received from the dear one who passed. When this is accomplished, the scrapbook and storyboard are given to the family.

Leader: "When we contemplate our gratitude for being able to share time, love, and wisdom with [*name*], it reminds us of the importance of staying current with all our loved ones. Let not a day go by without a declaration of love for those closest to you or a statement of gratitude for the gifts you receive from another, for we do not know when any of our lives will move through the doorway into the next experience. Let us use this time together today to remind ourselves that the ultimate transition from this life need not be unexpected. Indeed, each of us will take that step in our perfect time. We are better prepared to embrace it when we have kept our communication of love current, our amends complete, and our regrets handled.

"To conclude this celebration of the life of [*name*], let us open our awareness to the mystery of coming in and leaving from this existence. One way to describe this movement of life is to say that we left our true home to come to earth. Now [*name*] has returned home, as we all will when it is our time. We wish [*name*] blessings, peace, and love on his continued journey."

. *Conclusion* .

Ritual infuses all aspects of my life: my profession, my travels, my friendships, my home, my challenges, my spiritual practices, and my parenting. As you reach the end of this book, I hope it is the beginning of your experience with the power of ritual. When my children mirror my ceremonial tendencies, I realize how deeply ritual permeates my life experience. Here are two short personal stories about ritual and my children.

Melanie's Ritual

When my daughter Melanie was five years old she performed an original ritual with her babysitter. I returned home one evening, and the friend who was babysitting said everything had gone well and that Melanie had done her bedtime ritual as usual. Suspicious, I asked him exactly how she had done this bedtime ritual.

He said that Melanie had uncorked her sacred bottle and made wafting motions over the bottle with her eyes closed in spiritual contemplation. Having carried the invisible contents of the bottle over herself, she asked him, "What in the far off past are you grateful for?" A little taken aback, he was able to respond after a moment. She then followed that with several more questions about gratitude as well as a review of her "gratitude list."

This went on well past the normal bedtime with the little priestess wafting, asking, and sharing, all in respectful, sacred tones that the babysitter thought he should not interrupt. Finally, after finishing her holy business, she lay down to sleep. I told him that he had been the victim of an elaborate (but sacred) staying up scheme!

Michael's Ritual

My son, Michael lives with two college roommates, all serious students who enjoy each others' company. My son called one day and said that they wanted me to create a closing ritual for their "Roommate Appreciation Week." I was honored and sent them the following ritual to acknowledge friendship as it deepens, moving through the eras of their lives.

Roommate Appreciation Ritual

Materials:

      30 one inch by six inch strips of paper

      Glue and pens

      "Past" and "Future" signs with tape

      Good wine or another beverage

      Written future scenarios (as described below)

      Envelopes

Set up:

> Each roommate writes a detailed and positive scenario for themselves and the other roommates about what their life will be like on their 30th birthday. These biographies should be the greatest description that can be envisioned with lots of details and the healing of any challenging issues that are being experienced today.

To begin, each roommate takes ten strips of paper and, one at a time, completes this statement: "My life has changed because of you in this way." The first person to complete this statement takes a strip of paper and forms a circle with it, gluing it in place. The second person takes a strip of paper, completes the statement and connects their strip of paper to the first going through the center of the first circle. Continue linking strips of paper to make a paper chain of appreciation. Attach the "Past" and "Future" signs to each end of the chain, and hang it in a place where it will remind you of your contribution to each others' lives from the past, through the present, and into the future.

Next, read the scenarios you have written for each other, as well as for yourself. Take some time to discuss these dreams, and then seal them in an envelope to be kept until your thirtieth birthdays.

Finally, toast each other with wine or another beverage, and savor the present moment with your friends.

*I*t is my sincere desire that you find creative ways to deepen your life through ritual. When there is a challenge facing you, I hope you will create a ritual to empower yourself. When there is a great blessing, a life transition, a loss, a new beginning, or a completion that appears on your path, I hope you will think, "A ritual, that's what I need." When a friend has a baby, a move, a job change, or another life transition, I hope you will offer him a sacred ceremony to assist with the changes he is going through.

I wish you the deep satisfaction and contentment that comes when we live in harmony with the earth, her seasons, and the seasons of our own life.

Blessed be.

. Part Four .

The Wheels

The Wheels

*T*he Wheels illustrate the flow of time, space, and energy, each showing the different aspects of life that are celebrated by the rituals in this book. The meaning of an individual point on one wheel can be deepened by studying the same point on all other wheels. For example, if you consider the western point on the wheels, which is the fall equinox, you see that harvest, gifts, tributes, and retirement all are found on this point of the other wheels. The activities of turning within and feeling your emotions are also significant to this point. The West is a time of completion, the direction of the setting sun at the completion of a day. All the western points of the Wheels deepen these ideas of endings and accomplishment. The correspondence of ideas and energy is the same for any point on all the circles.

Another way of using the Wheels is to put yourself anywhere on the circumference of a Wheel and look directly across the circle. If you stand on the West, feeling the endings, harvest, and gratitude of this place on the Wheel, when you look across you will be reminded that there are new beginnings for you, accompanied by inspiration, enlightenment, and winds of change. You may also imagine yourself in the center of a circle and study the various energy and ideas flowing toward you from all directions.

✚

The Celtic Cross

A circle with a cross in it is the ancient symbol of our experience on earth. Known as the Celtic Cross, it can be found in ancient sites across Europe and Britain. As it was brought into the Christian era, it was modified slightly by extending the vertical bar downward beyond the circle.

In its most ancient form the circle represents all that exists. The horizontal bar is the flow of time and space. The vertical bar is the height and depth of the penetration of spirit, life, love, and wisdom in every moment. As the circle spins, we understand ourselves to be spiritual beings in the midst of physical time, space, and form, moment to moment, step by step.

Wheel of the Year .

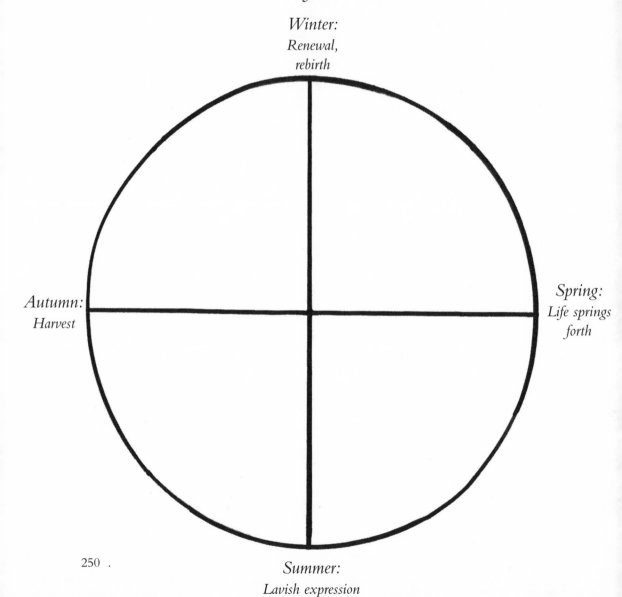

Winter:
*Renewal,
rebirth*

Spring:
*Life springs
forth*

Autumn:
Harvest

Summer:
Lavish expression

. *Wheel of Directions, Elements, Energies, and Symbols* .

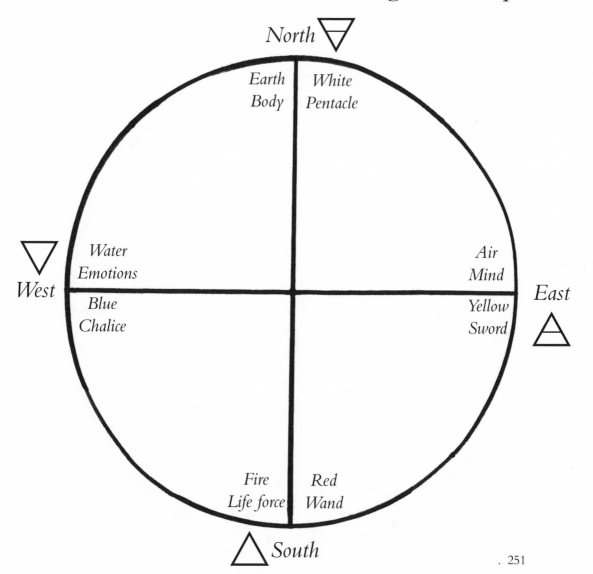

North

Earth
Body

White
Pentacle

West

Water
Emotions

Blue
Chalice

Air
Mind

Yellow
Sword

East

Fire
Life force

Red
Wand

South

. 251

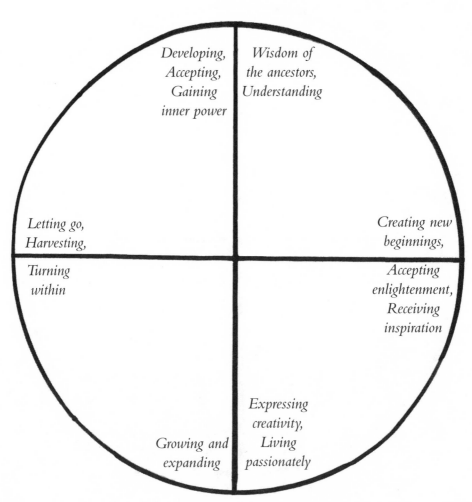

Developing, Accepting, Gaining inner power

Wisdom of the ancestors, Understanding

Letting go, Harvesting, Turning within

Creating new beginnings, Accepting enlightenment, Receiving inspiration

Growing and expanding

Expressing creativity, Living passionately

Wheel of the Hero's Journey

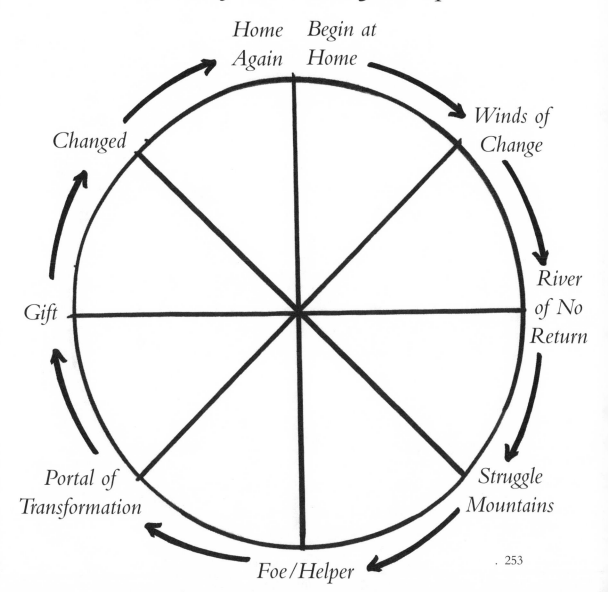

Home Again

Begin at Home

Winds of Change

River of No Return

Struggle Mountains

Foe / Helper

Portal of Transformation

Gift

Changed

. 253

Wheel of a Lifetime

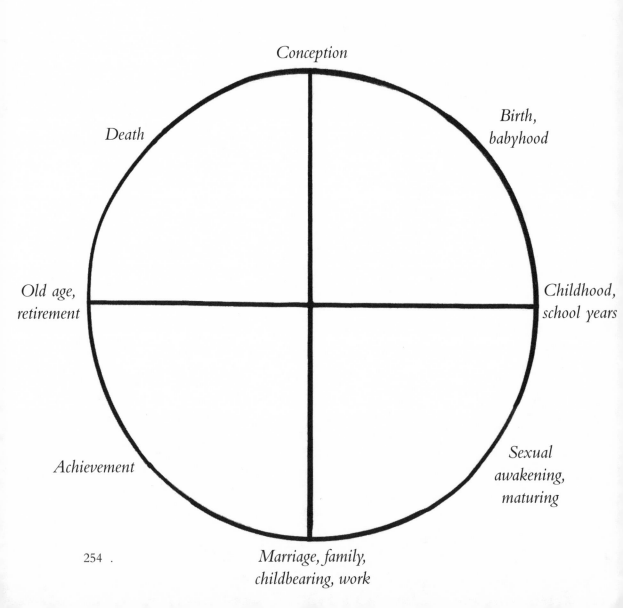

Conception

Birth,
babyhood

Death

Old age,
retirement

Childhood,
school years

Achievement

Sexual
awakening,
maturing

254 .

Marriage, family,
childbearing, work

Wheel of Life Passages

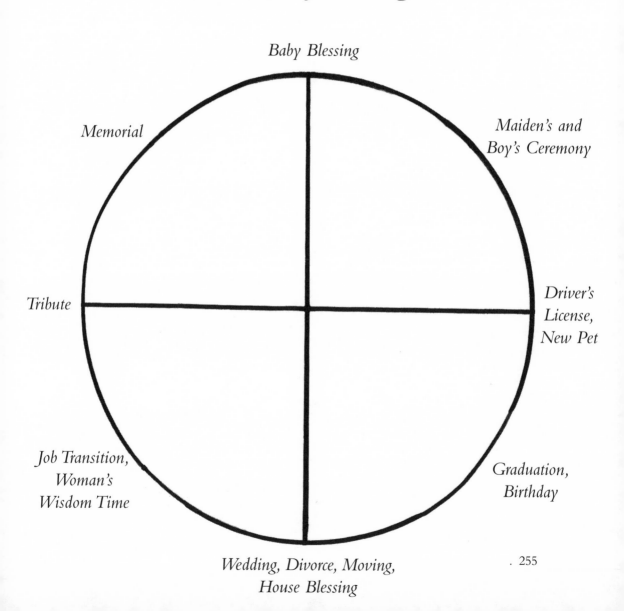

Baby Blessing

Maiden's and Boy's Ceremony

Memorial

Tribute

Driver's License, New Pet

Job Transition, Woman's Wisdom Time

Graduation, Birthday

Wedding, Divorce, Moving, House Blessing

Wheel of the Year Calendar .

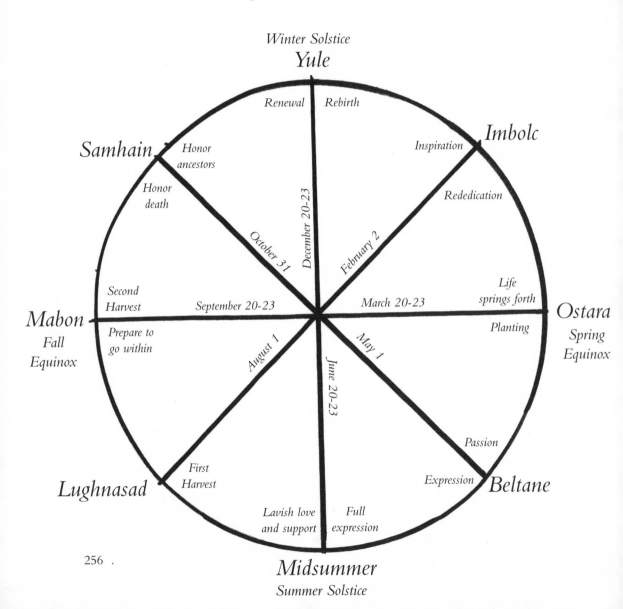

Birthday Wheel

Name: _____
Date: _____

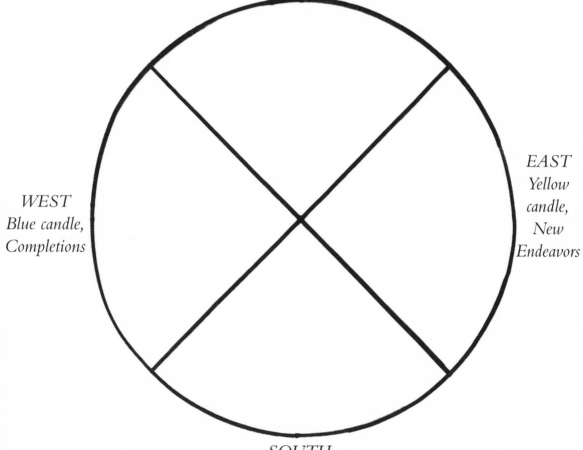

NORTH
White candle, Legacy

EAST
Yellow candle, New Endeavors

WEST
Blue candle, Completions

SOUTH
Red candle, Service

Unfolding Year Wheel

Name: _____

Date: _____

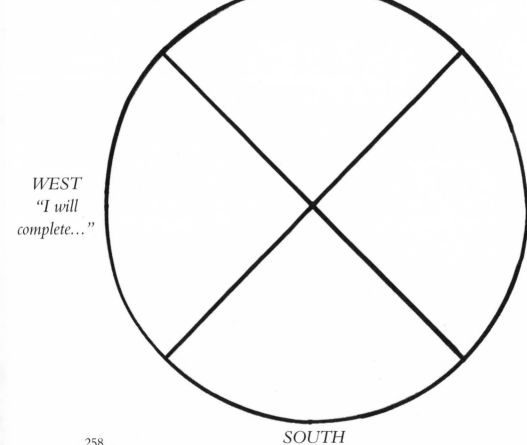

NORTH
"I will leave as a legacy…"

WEST
"I will complete…"

EAST
"I will begin…"

SOUTH
"I will serve…"

Job Transition Wheel

Name: _____

Date: _____

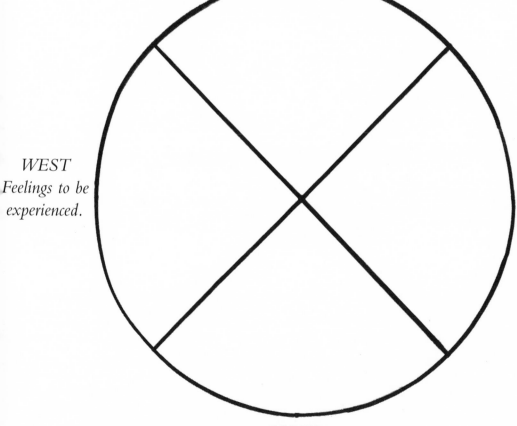

NORTH
Whole and complete state of being to be lived.

EAST
New endeavors to be expressed. New goals to be set.

WEST
Feelings to be experienced.

SOUTH
Skills to be developed. Support to be received. Work to be given.